£5.95

CW01668325

ALL CHANGE

Kingston, Surbiton & New Malden in the 19th Century

JUNE SAMPSON

Published by St Luke's Church, Kingston upon Thames
4 Burton Road
Kingston upon Thames

ISBN 0 9509958 0 0

Photoset in Century Schoolbook by Marion Cook
Artwork by Freddie Cook Design Associates
6 Burton Road
Kingston upon Thames, Surrey KT2 5TE

Printed and bound by
Simpson Drewett and Company Limited
70 Sheen Road
Richmond, Surrey TW9 1UF

Contents

KINGSTON HALL

Drawing by Freddie Cook based on an illustration in the British Library's Graingerised edition of Manning and Bray's History of Surrey.

Introduction

There is something irresistible about looking through a lighted window into someone else's world. Travelling at night by train or car, or walking along a street after dark, who can resist glancing in at any uncurtained windows as one passes by? The scenes inside are usually ordinary enough. What gives them their special appeal is their inaccessibility. Each is a separate, private world we cannot enter. We can only steal a look.

Local history is rather like that. As one journeys along, coping with the present and wondering about the future, there is something at once engrossing, re-assuring and instructive in trying to get glimpses of the past, and to see what other people in other times did with the self-same spot we are occupying now.

The aim of this book is to part the curtains on a lot of little windows to catch glimpses of life in Victorian Kingston – not as we might fondly imagine it was, but as it *truly* was, warts and all.

Some 18 years of spare-time searching through original sources in Kingston Borough Archives, the Public Record Office and private collections did something to unveil those windows. So did forays through the printed material in Kingston Heritage Centre's local history collection. But often the scenes they revealed were hazy, or curiously lifeless and unreal. The illumination of the windows, and the animation of those within, was achieved by reading literally thousands of the newspapers issued between the 1830's and the close of the century.

Nineteenth century newspapers are among the most important local history documents we have. To read them is to re-live past situations through people who were actually there, meticulously noting every detail.

Newspapers rarely carried pictures until after the turn of the century. To compensate, journalists reported in precise and vivid depth, using their command of language like the lens of a camera. This was particularly true of Kingston's two main papers, the *Surrey Comet* and the *Kingston and Surbiton News*.

The *Surrey Comet* was founded in 1854 and, now Surrey's oldest surviving newspaper, has continued without a break ever since. The Kingston and Surbiton News was established in 1882 by former Comet editor, William Drewett. It continued until 1900, when Drewett joined forces with the Comet's owner, Mary Ann Knapp. His newspaper then became the *Midweek Comet,* and has continued to be published as such on every Wednesday since.

Drewett lived all his life in Kingston and described local events as a journalist from 1863 until his death in 1928.

"My desire is to be as accurate as possible; for newspaper reports of the present are important factors in the making of history for the future," he declared in one of his editorials.

I agree. That is why so much of this book is based on newspaper research.

Drewett has long been my favourite guide to Victorian Kingston and it is appropriate that this volume has been printed by his descendant, Peter Drewett, who, as a partner in the firm Simpson Drewett, is maintaining his family's long connection with publishing.

The book represents a labour of love for Kingston in general and for its parish church of St Luke in particular. It arose out of St Luke's centenary in 1983, and all proceeds from it will go to the building and maintenance of the Swinnerton Hall. This, named in memory of St Luke's first vicar, is being built alongside the church to enrich the pastoral, community and social activities among 6,000 parishioners.

Individuals have donated time and professional expertise. Local firms whose committment to Kingston goes far beyond their business success, have joined with Kingston Lottery Fund in meeting the cost of printing and binding. Thus every penny from sales can go straight to the hall fund.

It is difficult to convey the depth of my gratitude to those who have given so unstintingly. There are three in particular without whose encouragement the task of writing might not have been finished: Elizabeth Stazicker, deputy county archivist for Surrey, and a member of St Luke's congregation; Joan Wakeford, acknowledged as Kingston's most respected amateur local historian; and Margaret Vaughan-Lewis, archivist to the Royal Borough. They performed the time-consuming task of reading the unprocessed manuscript, and provided invaluable advice and information. Joan Wakeford also compiled the index, a notoriously onerous task. Marion Gray researched the Census Returns for Elm Road. Marion Hinton, Colin Cornish and Anne Baker provided unfailing help and patience at Kingston Heritage Centre.

As far as production is concerned, no words can adequately express my thanks to Freddie and Marion Cook of the respected Kingston firm, Freddie Cook Design Associates. Marion gave up her leisure time, and often worked far into the night, to accomplish the typesetting. Freddie was responsible for the artwork and design. Both made this enormous contribution on a purely voluntary basis for love of St Luke's Church, which Marion has attended all her life and of which Freddie is Vicar's Warden. Without them this book could never have become a reality.

Immense generosity was also shown by two of my *Surrey Comet* colleagues, Jeffrey Edwards and David Cosh, and by freelance photographer Roy Cook. They freely gave of their time and expertise to provide pictures.

J.S.

SURBITON PLACE

Surbiton – A Scandalous Suburb

Trim little semis, tidy little gardens, bourgeous little minds . . . the national image of Surbiton is, solely through the sound of its name, firmly rooted in the popular concept of 20th century commuterland suburbia between the wars.

Historically, the truth is very different. Surbiton is of ancient origin. Furthermore, its name was once synonymous with sex – and illicit sex at that!

Though the town as it is today grew after the coming of the railway in 1838, Surbiton was in existence at least as early as the 12th century. For example, records detailed by Alfred Heales in his *Records of Merton Priory,* published in 1898, show that in 1179 some 20 men of Surbiton, led by John Hog, leased land to the prior and Convent of Merton. John Hog, incidentally, was probably one of the family of millers whose name is immortalised in the Hogsmill River.

During its early centuries, Surbiton was a mere hamlet with farming and, later, brickmaking the major occupations. Some, however, used it for quite a different purpose. Though only a carriage drive from Kingston, Twickenham and London, it was an isolated spot, bounded by the wild acres of Surbiton Common and the solitary, marshy banks of the Thames. Here seemingly blameless gentlemen could indulge themselves with ladies of pleasure without family or friends being any the wiser.

By the early 18th century, the word Surbiton meant a nudge and a wink, as indicated by this extract from *Woodward's Miscellany,* published in 1731:

"One Part there is adjacent to this Town,
Which by the Name of Surbiton is known;
A Private Place, long mark'd to entertain
Kept Mistresses e'er since great William's Reign.
When Ev'ning comes, out from the Garden Door,
Each takes a separate path to air his W...e.
One shall with blackcurl'd Spaniel beat the Fields,

Or take the Pleasure that Common yields;
Another to the Thames shall steer away,
To see the finny Race both sport and play,
'till satisfy'd with Pleasure home they turn.
In Love they revel, and at Night they burn."

Old habits die hard. The *Surrey Comet* of September 22, 1883 carries complaints of "disgraceful nightly scenes by disorderly females in Portsmouth Road", and at least as late as the 1960's it was said that the Surbiton end of Portsmouth Road was the place to go in search of hired pleasure!

The advent of railways transformed Surbiton from an isolated hill top hamlet to a fashionable new town, first known as Kingston-on-Railway, or New Kingston. The first man to make a significant step in the creation of the new town was Christopher Terry, and his contribution was to die at precisely the right moment. This might seem a negative role, but he spent much time drawing up his will, and without it today's Surbiton would never have materialised in the way it did.

Mr Terry had made his money as a merchant with important business connections on the coast of Sumatra. In 1815 he built himself a comfortable home near Kingston, surrounded by 150 acres of fine, level land and set himself up as a gentleman farmer. His estate was known as Maple Farm. His house stood near the site now occupied by the Claremont Hall in Maple Road, and survived as Maple Lodge long after the farm had gone.

In local history books, Mr Terry is a mere shadow; but a vivid picture of him and the kind of life lived by an old-fashioned country gentleman of the period emerges in the will he made in 1833, five years before his death. He was evidently a good employer, careful of the welfare of his employees, whether past or present. They had well furnished rooms of their own and, from the language of the will, it would appear that the relationship was almost that of affectionate friends rather than master and servants. There are bequests of £50 a year, or £500 in cash, "to my faithful and good servant, Anne Richardson, for her long service, and to my faithful and good servant, William Cooper."

William Cooper is recalled by William Ayliffe in his *Memories of an Octagenarian.* He was the butler who, on Mr Terry's orders, kept a supply of cakes and cream in his pantry for the local youngsters who always found a welcome at Maple Farm. The will also reveals Mr Terry's fondness for going out round his farm to shoot fowl for dinner; his habit of ambling round the grounds on a bay pony; his liking for a game of backgammon and for the bamboo furniture which must have reminded him of Sumatra.

Mr Terry was 93 when he died at Maple Farm in January 1838, the faithful William Cooper at his side.

"It is my particular desire that my funeral be private and at little expense . . . no pageantary, but to have a hearse with two horses and two coaches if necessary. My remains to be deposited in the grave of my wife in Kingston Churchyard," he directs in his will.

He had determined there should be no arguments over his property by leaving instructions "to sell all my estate to any person or persons willing to become the purchaser or purchasers thereof." The proceeds were then to be divided between the beneficiaries.

It was little short of a miracle that such a site should have become available just at the time the London and Southampton Railway was opening a station close by. Yet there was no rush to purchase, and when the land was auctioned, a block of 100 acres went for what *The Times* considered to be the surprisingly low price of £10,500. Of all the wealthy and supposedly shrewd men living in and around this part of Surrey, only one seems to have realised the land's enormous potential. That man was Thomas Pooley. It was he who bought the greater part of the Terry estate and it was he who conceived the idea of creating the town we now know as Surbiton around the new railway.

What happened to him would appear to be far more scandalous than the centuries of naughtiness on Surbiton Common. The facts have never been published before. They are hidden in massive bundles of chancery documents (numbers C14 280/25) in the Public Record Office.

Census Returns, street directories and the Register of Births, Deaths and Marriages indicate that the Pooleys came originally from Cornwall. Early in the 19th century, like so many others at that time, they made the big decision to leave the country and try their luck in London. They settled in St Luke's, then a comparatively new Parish in the Finsbury district. Their home was in Old Street, a teeming centre where every building housed a different trade or craft. Here Thomas Pooley earned and saved sufficient to make him a man of some substance. Enough, at any rate, to enable him and his wife, Jane, to leave the crowded din of Old Street for the comparative peace of Kingston.

By 1838 the Kingston rate books show him to be running three malthouses, and his son Alexander a fourth, situated near the Kingston riverside between what is now South Lane and Woodbines Avenue. The chancery documents reveal also that he owned three valuable cargo vessels – the *Agnes,* the *Elizabeth* and the *Mahon Castle* – working international routes.

Kingston in the 19th century was largely managed by men with little knowledge of the world beyond the borough boundaries. According to chroniclers of the time, they had fought off the London and Southampton Railway in order to protect the town's coaching and inn-keeping activities, and lacked the vision, as did many others at that early stage, to see that the new railways had not only come to stay, but would revolutionise life as they knew it.

Thomas Pooley had been around. He shrewdly surmised that railways would kill coaching and, more important to him, the town's long and prosperous malting industry. It was time to look for a new career. Thus was born his dream of creating a new town, beautifully designed for, in his own words, "a great number of houses of various descriptions and sizes, suitable for the occupation of persons of various means and circumstances." The heart of the town was to be its station, and it was Pooley himself who decided to call it Kingston-upon-Railway.

That is not a very pleasing name now, but at the time the word 'railway' held the glamour and challenge of a brand new age.

Within weeks of purchasing the Terry lands, a London consortium made him a cash offer of £120,000 for the estate. This would have given him a sizable instant profit with no further effort, but he refused it on the spot. He had a dream to fulfil.

The extraordinary thing about the birth of this new town was that it was the work of one man. Thomas Pooley drew up the basic plans, engaged the architect, hired the builders, conferred with engineers and created new employment for hundreds of labourers. He also superintended the entire operation, moving swiftly from site to site, ablaze with enthusiasm. His dream took shape with amazing rapidity. At the time he bought Maple Farm, a bumper crop of oats was being reaped. Eighteen months later, those oatfields had been covered by roads and 200 houses had been built.

It was too much for many Kingstonians of substance. They determined this upstart must go. There would seem to be many reasons for this. One was that a relative newcomer, probably rough in speech and manners, should make such sweeping changes in their parish. It must have been painful to see that, through their own lack of perspicacity, it was Pooley and not they who seemed to be on the way to certain fortune. Then there was the scope of his enterprise, details of which had been printed and distributed over a wide area. It was obvious that Pooley's Kingston-on-Railway was not going to be simply a bland suburb. It was going to have markets, loading wharves and other fine commercial facilities, as well as houses of a style and elegance never before seen in Kingston. What sort of devastation would that wreak on trade and industry in the old town?

Finally, Pooley and his relations seem to have been, in Victorian parlance, very much from the lower orders. Pooley himself, for all his remarkable energy and initiative, emerges from the documents as a man of humble origins with a painful lack of finesse. He did not even know the date of his birth. In 1844, for instance he states in the chancery papers that he is "54, 56 or 58, I cannot say which."

Then there was his relative by marriage, William Wadbrook. Wadbrook owned extensive maltings in the Portsmouth Road area and his daughter, Jane, had married Pooley's son, Alexander, in 1837. Wadbrook had also invested substantially in Pooley's grand design.

That a man like this should be involved in the building of a town intended primarily for the higher classes could have caused resentment.

The Wadbrooks had been in Kingston for centuries, mainly as watermen. Local court records, census returns and newspaper references indicate that they were unpolished people with a rough turn of speech. Nevertheless, they showed great shrewdness and success in business and the ratebooks show that by 1777 George Wadbrook had built The Elms, a handsome house that still gives a touch of distinction to the Surbiton Road/Portsmouth Road corner. George makes a brief but striking appearance in the Kingston Bailiffs' Minutes, which record his fine "for cursing and swearing ten times during time of divine service."

The Elms was subsequently inherited by George's son, William. He became a man of considerable means, but made no attempt to bow to social convention. He is remembered thus in the Diamond Jubilee commemoration issue of the *Surrey Comet,* published in June 1897:

> "The house adjoining the entrance gates of Woodbines Park was in the occupation of a well-known Kingston character who went about in corduroy knee breeches and maltster's cap. He was considered in those days a man of great wealth, having five stars to his name as a holder of shares in the East India Company – each star denoting the sum of £20,000. He was in the habit of carrying a large roll of bank notes in his pocket – from one thousand to several thousand pounds. One hot summer's day, while busily engaged in nailing up his peach trees, a son of Captain Robinson, who lived at Woodbines, thinking him to be the gardener, gave him half-a-crown, remarking: 'You've a hot job there, old man.' The old gentleman thanked him for the money and promptly pocketed it. A few days later he met young Robinson and asked whether he remembered giving him half-a-crown a few days before. 'I never forget a kindness,' he said, and pulled out

a wad of notes peeled off one for £50 and gave it to him – to the young man's great astonishment."

Pooley and Wadbrook were probably embarrassing enough to those with social pretensions. Even worse was John Selfe, an eccentric brickmaker who owned so much land at the top of Surbiton Hill that the area was generally known as Selfe's Park.

The Selfes had been painters and plumbers in Thames Street, Kingston since 1772. Their yard was an old cobbled backwater called Fountain Court because of the spring of pure water which welled up in its centre. In fact, Fountain Court survived until the 1930's, when it was demolished and replaced by Lyons Teashop. The Selfes were good enough for old Kingston. In fact, Mr Harry Selfe was Bailiff (the former equivalent of Mayor) three times. When it came to New Kingston it was a different matter.

Harry Selfe, who for years had sold water from his well for a halfpenny a bucket, decided to market water on a grander scale. He formed a new firm, Harry Selfe and Co., and leased a riverside site from Pooley at £35 a year. Here he planned to establish waterworks that would supply water on tap to the new town.

Meanwhile his son, John, had acquired several acres of Surbiton Hill, where some of Surbiton's most elegant houses were to be built. What must have made it worse, as far as the jealous ones were concerned was that the Selfes were related by marriage to the hated Pooleys and the despised Wadbrooks. John Selfe married William Wadbrook's eldest daughter, Harriott, making him Alexander Pooley's brother-in-law. Thus it was that John Selfe, like Thomas Pooley, appears to have been ruined by those who considered themselves socially superior.

This, then, was the background as Thomas Pooley toiled round the clock to get his new town completed. By the time of the Census in 1841 he had left his maltings in Portsmouth Road and moved with his wife to the first house to be completed in Claremont Crescent (now known simply as The Crescent). To mark his new status, he acquired two house servants and styled himself on documents as 'independent'. At the same time, as also shown by the 1841 Census, his 28-year-old son, Alexander, became one of the first residents of what we now know as Victoria Road. He took the first house in Victoria Terrace, a row of Georgian-style town houses that still survive at the station end of Victoria Road, but have long since been converted into shops.

From 1840, Alexander seems to have given up all other employment to help his father in the creation of the new town, describing himself as a 'gentleman' instead of, as previously, a brewer. By this time Thomas, after two years long struggle, was in need of help. The full venom of Kingston had been turned on him, crushing his plans, delaying his schedule and forcing him to borrow heavily from Coutts' Bank.

Exactly what was done to sabotage Pooley? It was never revealed openly. But one can read much between the lines of, for example, this extract from the Kingston Council minutes of November 9, 1840:

> "Instructions were given to the Town Clerk to give Mr Pooley notice that his application to Parliament for an act for creating a new market in the New Town would be opposed and the Mayor, Mr Mercer, Mr James Nightingale, Mr Shrubsole and Mr Ald Fricker were appointed a committee for watching the proceedings with reference to such application."

At the same time, a petition was sent to Parliament, vehemently opposing Mr Pooley.

Kingston had no proper corn market at this time, and Kingston's commercial leaders were enraged that Pooley was about to upstage them. As soon as they heard of his plan for such a market they sent a memo to Kingston Council, recorded in the minutes, that they "erect a market for the sale of corn and grain in bulk, to be pitched in the Market Place in lieu of the present sample market."

The plan was never carried out – presumably because Pooley's was not, either.

There is no doubt that many destructive moves were made against Pooley. Even the dignified *Times* newspaper, not normally given to parochial tittle tattle, was moved to deplore the scandalous treatment meted out to him.

"Great credit is due to the good taste of Mr Pooley, as well as to his enterprise and unceasing exertions to carry out his design," it remarked on August 8, 1840. "It is to be regretted he has met with considerable opposition, and has had to encounter prejudice, both of communities and individuals, and to contend single-handed against a host of selfish feeling and interested opposition."

Local personalities of the time refer to Pooley only in slighting terms, as a feckless speculator who built a lot of rubbish before plunging into ruin. Indeed, that is how he still appears to anyone who studies the standard local history books of the 19th century. Frederick Merryweather, in his celebrated *Half a Century of Kingston History,* describes the Pooley houses as "stuccoed villas, pretentious in design and capricious in style." Brayley and Britton, in their *History of Surrey*, published in 1843, describe Pooley's buildings as "a somewhat capricious style of architecture."

Few Pooley houses have survived the wave of re-development that has swept Surbiton in recent years. Those that have are graceful buildings, with more than a touch of Regency elegance. Good examples survive on the east side of Claremont Road, opposite Claremont Gardens. Certainly they are more attractive than most of the houses put up after Pooley had gone. By "capricious" the critics really meant "varied", for Pooley was endeavouring to construct a town of pleasingly individual buildings, rather than the usual rows of dull uniformity. He was also laying out elegant crescents and avenues instead of stereotyped streets. At any rate, he took the trouble to engage one of the foremost architects of the day. He was Harvey Elmes, who before his tragically early death had so impressed the Prince Consort with his work that he was awarded a special gold medal.

Elmes had drawn up designs for a corn exchange and a cattle, hay and general market in New Kingston, and building had actually begun under his direction, when the project was halted through the machinations of Pooley's opponents. He had also designed a church and a vicarage, for which Pooley had earmarked the site and the money.

Disaster struck in January 1842 when Coutts Bank, who had loaned him £16,000, refused to lend him any more. Creditors closed in on every side and soon he was in danger of his life from crew members of his ships, the *Agnes* and *Elizabeth,* who had not been paid.

Then began an extraordinary saga which makes the mass of documents in the Public Record Office read like a Victorian melodrama. There are some 800 of these papers, each the size of a hearth mat and tightly hand-written in faded, often indecipherable inks. They represent Pooley's two-year battle in Chancery against more than 20 defendants – a battle which was lost before it had begun, considering the formidable oppositon.

It is important to stress that none of the defendants was guilty of breaking the law. The prestigious banks, solicitors and other professional men involved were too sophisticated for that. Instead, they were able to use their talents, and their very considerable influence, to outwit the unschooled Pooley. They triumphed handsomely in the end. Their only unpleasant surprise was that it took so long. Pooley simply would not give in until he had literally been banished from the face of the British earth. Even then his son, Alexander, kept up the vain struggle for a time.

Coutts and the other bodies involved wanted to get rid of Pooley but retain his Kingston-on-Railway. This was partly due to action by his Kingston foes. Pooley's solicitors had, without his knowledge, written to Coutts warning them of "bad feeling existing between Mr Pooley and certain parties in Kingston who will always endeavour to injure the property as long as Mr Pooley is connected with it."

In court, the solicitors stated that in 1842, when Pooley had been forced to suspend building work, many of the partly-completed houses were vandalised to such an extent by mysterious hands that they eventually had to be demolished and re-built. Thus Pooley's nameless enemies were able to reduce the value of his assets and so hasten his end. At the same time, Coutts and his other main creditors had to prevent his going bankrupt before they were in possession of his land once and for all.

According to Pooley's allegations in Chancery, they embarked on an extraordinary hole-and-corner action to achieve their aim.

Pooley always maintained that his estate at Kingston-on-Railway was more than sufficient in value to meet all his debts and secure further loans, and later events proved this to be so. Coutts refused to accept his claim, denigrating the value of the land and the notion that the railway gave it any extra advantage – though their attitude, it must be said, was very different once it had passed into their possession. At last, Pooley offered to dispose of all his holdings to Coutts in exchange for a life annuity of £1,000. Coutts refused.

By June 1842 Pooley was so desperate he agreed to hand over his holdings in the new town to trustees appointed by his principal creditors. In exchange, he alleged, they made a gentlemen's agreement to pay him £5 a week. This was his sole income, and he found himself obliged to do what so many financially embarrassed Englishmen have done: flee across the Channel to eke out an existence in France. He settled in drab anonymity in Boulogne until November 1843.

Then he received a rude shock in the form of a curt letter informing him that his £5 a week would no longer be paid. He was further told that his son, Alexander, was dangerously ill. Pooley was advised to return to England immediately, but in strict secrecy because of the seamen still seeking his blood. He was not to come to London Bridge, which would be too dangerous, but to go to Greenwich and from there travel into Surrey, as there was no writ against him in that county. Accommodation was arranged for him at his solicitor's house in Old Kent Road, which at that time was in Surrey.

He obeyed these instructions, returning to Britain in January 1844. According to his statement in Chancery, that month was a nightmare in which mounting pressure was put upon him to sign away all claims on New Kingston. Finally, when threatened with jail, he declared he would rather that than be robbed of his rights. Fists flew in the solicitor's office and bodies hit the floor before a coach was called to take him to White Cross Street Prison. Pooley had been bundled into the coach, and was about to be driven off, when his daughter-in-law, Jane, arrived weeping to say that her sick husband had been dragged from his bed against doctor's orders and arrested for one of his father's debts, for which he had stood surety.

Says the official complaint, filed on Pooley's behalf in the Chancery Court:

> "So distressed at the thought of the state to which your orator and his son had been reduced, and being wholly without the means of existence, and being unable to rely upon his solicitors, who had it in their power by informing any of your orator's creditors of his arrest to keep your orator in prison, he determined to execute the said deed, and therefore in great distress, and with tears, requested to return to the legal offices."

Back at the offices he found his sick son, in sheriff's custody. Then followed a lengthy wait while the necessary documents were engraved at the stationers. When they finally came, Pooley again thought better of signing away his new town, and tried to leave. After a violent altercation, it was realised he had had nothing to eat or drink all day, and one of the solicitors and two of the clerks were instructed to take him to a nearby inn.

The refreshments they gave him were wholly of a liquid kind. Pooley claims he was "prevailed upon to drink several glasses of spirit, and stayed several hours, until in a state of great excitement from liquor and the events of the day" he finally signed.

In the sober light of next day, he claimed he had been intoxicated, and not in full possession of his senses, when he scrawled his signature. He refused to acknowledge the deed as his own voluntary act and, dogged to the end, filed complaints in the Chancery Court which dragged on for more than two years.

A final blow was the death of Alexander's young wife, Jane, at the age of 28. She died in 1846, leaving three small children. Her death was doubtless hastened by the crash of the Pooleys and the humiliation of seeing the public destruction of their reputation. For, in 1844, Coutts Bank had taken possession of most of the new town. Alexander Road, so proudly named by Thomas Pooley in honour of his son, was changed to Victoria Road, Wadbrook Terrace, a row of 20 villas named as a tribute to William Wadbrook, had its name removed and became just a series of numbers in what Pooley had called Railway Road, but which his successors re-named Claremont Road.

A particularly bitter pill was that John Stevens, an architect and surveyor who had purported to be Pooley's confidant throughout his troubles, was the man who supervised the annihilation of every detail that might remind posterity of Pooley. Each day, on Coutts' behalf,

Stevens drove from London in a four-in-hand and toured his firm's newly-acquired domain in lordly style. Even the name of kindly old Christopher Terry was lost to posterity. Terry's Lane was re-styled Maple Road, a name it has retained to this day.

If only the Pooleys had been able to stay the course! By 1853 land in the new town of Surbiton, as it had been re-named, was fetching £500 an acre. By 1854 it was fetching £1,000.

So ended the Pooley dream. Thomas Pooley vanishes from the scene after 1846, his Chancery proceedings suspended in mid-air. There appears to be no record of his death in the national registers, so the assumption must be that he died abroad. Alexander battled vainly through the courts during the late 1840's and early '50's until he, too, disappeared. But an article on the art of brewing and distilling, written in 1876 by Thomas Alexander Pooley (the name of Alexander's son) and a reference to the will of a man of the same name in the Brewer's Journal of January 1903, suggests that the family returned to a trade which they understood far better than speculative development and high finance.

Certainly Pooley was foolish. He might also have been a rogue. Nevertheless, it would be appropriate if there was a Pooley Road, or some other memorial to this extraordinary man.

However, Surbiton has chosen to forget its original creator. The only honourable epitaph he has are editorials in *The Times* of 1840, when he was still in confident charge of Surbiton's development. This is an extract from the issue of October 22:

> "Nothing in the history of railway improvements has been more extraordinary than the creation of this singular new town. On the spot where, last harvest two years, a large crop of oats was reaped, now stand rows of handsome houses, terraces, villas, Swiss and other ornamental cottages, a splendid hotel and tavern, with assembly, billiard and coffee rooms, and other useful and ornamental buildings; while gasworks, waterworks and other necessary adjuncts to the health and comfort of a town are about to be commenced, as also an episcopalian church, and a Wesleyan meeting house. Roads intersect in an agreeble manner the entire estate, which lies between, and is bounded by, the Surbiton Road, which leads from Kingston to Ewell on the east, and by the Kingston to Leatherhead road on the west. The beautiful trees which decorated the former park now embellish the undulating grounds of this extremely picturesque town, which commands from the south east portion of the demesne extensive views over Claremont, Hampton Court, Richmond

Park and other charming places which surround it on every side . . . . In addition to any detached houses which are dotted about the parklike scenery of the new town a large crescent, named after her Majesty's Palace at Claremont, is laid out for villas in pairs and detached, some of which are already inhabited, and foundations for others are being daily excavated. The wide and handsome roads that meander through the town are hourly frequented by the fashionable equestrians and characters of the neighbourhood."

On August 8 *The Times* had declared of New Kingston:

"It is at present in its infancy, it being little more than 18 months since the first house was erected. So vigorously, however, has the growth of the place proceeded, and so excellent are the plans laid down to secure its success, that there is no doubt of its coming much more rapidly to maturity than towns and cities usually have done. The site of the town covers a space of about 100 acres – a site which exceeds the site of the old town of Kingston nearly four-fold. It is in the form of an angle, bounded by the railroad, the road from Kingston to Epsom and the Portsmouth Road. The railroad passes in front of the new town, having it on the right hand from London. Streets and a crescent, which will consist of nearly 900 houses, are already laid down and about 200 houses, including a large and commodious tavern are already erected. Many of them are inhabited. There is a line of wharfs for the loading and unloading of goods and coals already established along the railroad, and a busy scene of industry is already to be contemplated. Brickmaking is in operation, and many hundred labourers are to be seen in active employment. The value of the property on which these operations are going on has increased to an incalculable extent, in some cases to an extent almost beyond belief, and the land is becoming more valuable every day . . . on some situations the prospects are magnificent, embracing the parks of Hampton, Bushy, Claremont and other places, the Castle of Windsor and the spire of Harrow . . . Great credit is due to the good taste of Mr Pooley, the founder of the place, as well as to his enterprise and unceasing exertions to carry out his design . . . when it is taken into account that all the works at this place have been planned and directed by one individual, and that the whole expense of the operation has been defrayed by one purse, the rapidity with which the whole has proceeded, and the judgment by which it has been conducted, are surprising."

Meanwhile John Selfe had settled at Surbiton as a brick and tile maker. His home was Little Elmers, which still stands near the junction of Surbiton Hill Road and St Mark's Hill. One of his brickfields was nearby in Ewell Road, on the spot formerly occupied by an old windmill that had been a picturesque landmark for miles around. John Selfe was evidently an admirer of his shrewd old father-in-law William Wadbrook (he gave three of his children the name Wadbrook) and, like him, was a plain-speaking individualist, proud of his family and of the fact that one of the most valuable sites in the area was known as Selfe's Park.

However, he was dealing with opponents superior in education and social class, and gradually he seems to have been eased out of his lands. In the 1850's, for example, Mr William Walter, owner of Surbiton Hill House, found a way of eventually parting John Selfe from his windmill field. Mr Walter was Kingston's borough treasurer and a noted solicitor, and he filed a bill in Chancery to compel John Selfe to stop firing bricks on the grounds that it constituted a nuisance. He won, thus preventing Selfe from carrying on his livelihood on that spot. The action also made life difficult for other brickmakers in Britain because the case was thereafter used as a precedent. It is hardly surprising that, prevented from using his brick kilns, Selfe was eventually persuaded to sell the site. It is even less surprising that the lucky purchaser was William Walter. His purchase made him a handsome profit, for the houses in South Bank Terrace, plus five imposing villas facing Ewell Road, were then built on Selfe's field and the orchard adjoining it.

William Walter also profited from another man who, like the unfortunate Thomas Pooley, let his taste for elegance run away with his capital. He was William Clerk, developer of some of the most imposing houses in Surbiton.

His bankruptcy in 1855 was no misfortune for Mr Walter who, as chief creditor, was able to claim most of the estate. William Clerk has been forgotten, but some of the beautiful residences he built in the Oak Hill area remain as his anonymous memorial.

But to return to John Selfe. As with the Pooleys, precise reasons for his ruin are still obscure, but over the years he seems to have been cheated out of land and property. The gentry of Surbiton administered a last twist of the screw by petitioning the council to change the name of Selfe's Park. They got their way. It was re-named Surbiton Hill Park, and has remained so to this day. However, for some years afterwards there was a Selfe's Road in the area. That disappeared when one of Surbiton's richest residents had a confrontation with Mr Selfe and in revenge applied successfully to have Selfe's Road re-named. That was Mr Daniel Nicols, owner and creator of the Regent House estate, after which Regent Road is named.

John Selfe may have been down, but he was by no means out. He resolutely refused to leave an area he felt was righfully his, and to the end of his days he kept up a continuous campaign to publicise the wrongs done to him. As the local newspapers throughout the 1870's and 1880's show, there was scarcely a court hearing, or a commissioners' meeting, or a public gathering in Surbiton which he did not interrupt to state his case. As he did not worry about making a spectacle of himself, he was able to cause considerable embarrassment, as well as mirth.

One of his more spectacular gestures was to have posters printed and prominently displayed in Surbiton and Kingston. One of them is preserved in Kingston's local history collection, and John Selfe's personality comes blazing through.

> "WANTED, AN HONEST LAWYER!" declares the heading. "I, John Selfe, believing there are good and true men to be found in the law profession, want to find a man willing to make an agreement with me for his service to investigate certain transactions, wherein the parties I have employed have, by connivance, collusion, fraud and trickery, with others, wilfully, maliciously and wickedly robbed me of my money and wrongfully taken forcible possession of my properties. I am willing to give one thousand pounds to have certain works faithfully carried out. If my complaint is not thoroughly looked into by the Law Profession generally, particularly by the Law Protection Society and Law Associate, it will become a lasting disgrace and reflection on the whole body of lawyers, and a precedent whereby lawyers may rob and plunder people of their property with impunity . . . I hope and trust that all people who hear of this serious complaint will do all in their power to aid and assist me to bring to light the wicked and disgraceful transactions that I have been subject to for years, and put a stop to the wholesale plundering system that is practised with impunity at the present time by wicked lawless laywers. For further particulars apply to Mr John Selfe, Surbiton Hill Park, Kingston, Surrey; Shrublands Estate, Southborough Hill, Surbiton and other freehold land unencumbered. This is NO SHAM advertisement, but a reality."

Poor John Selfe. When he died in 1899, his estate only amounted to £21. 15s. 7d. Now he lies in a simple grave in Hook Churchyard.

Snobbery seems to have been a mainspring of 19th century Surbiton. One example, previously mentioned, was the re-naming of Selfe Park and Selfe Road. Another occurred in 1867, when the residents of George Street sought permission to change the name to Burdett Road, in honour of the Baroness Burdett Coutts, one of the wealthiest women in England and a great benefactress in the neighbourhood. The Surbiton Improvement Commissioners were shocked by such temerity. George Street had been planned by Thomas Pooley to house the labouring classes, and was tucked away discreetly from the view of the gentry. That such a road should bear the name of the Baroness was unthinkable and the request was refused even though, as the *Surrey Comet* reported, "attention was called to the fact that the locality had greatly improved in respectability and that an orderly class of people now live there." It was also pointed out that rents there had been raised to no less than 1s. 6d. a week. To no avail. When the name of George Street *was* changed, it was to Cottage Grove, so there should be no mistaking the class of place it was.

What became of tough old William Wadbrook? Nothing and nobody could vanquish him. Public derision left him unmoved and he was too astute to suffer from the ruin of his sons-in-law.

He even had the spirit to weather almost total blindness and the early death of his two daughters. Jane, as we have seen, died at 28. Harriett, married to John Selfe, died at only 35. William, meanwhile, lived to be 91 and kept working until his death at The Elms in May, 1867. In the Census Returns of 1861, he is described as "aged 84, maltster employing nine men."

An equally tough character was Sarah Langley of Southborough Lodge. Her husband, Thomas, had this beautiful house designed by the famous architect, John Nash, in 1808. The views from its windows were so breathtaking, looking out uninterruptedly to Hampton Court, that as houses were built in the area he insisted they remained without any upper storeys while he was alive – a fact recorded by Rowley Richardson in his *Surbiton History*.

Langley's house was surrounded by the magnificent acres of Southborough Farm and when he died his widow, though well into her seventies, refused to give up. She took over the reins of management and seems to have been justifiably proud of her success. In the Census Returns for 1851, when she was 85, she is described as "a landed proprietress, farming 200 acres, employing ten men." The Returns also show she had a butler, footman, cook, lady's maid, two housemaids and a coachman.

When Sarah Langley died in 1854, a nephew inherited the estate.

He was Charles Corkran, a dashing gentleman who enjoyed his wealth to the full. He was a splendid cricketer, captaining Oxford while at University, and one of the first players selected to represent the gentlemen of England when the annual contest of Gentlemen versus Players was instituted.

Captain Corkran left Southborough Lodge to settle in nearby Long Ditton. He died there in 1885 and is buried in St Mary's churchyard. But the name of Corkran Road is his best-known memorial. Southborough Lodge remains, lovely as ever, but its farm and park were sold off for building during the latter half of the 19th century to form today's Southborough estate. Thomas and Sarah Langley, meanwhile, are remembered in the names of Langley Road and Langley Avenue.

Surbiton Goes Ahead

With the Pooley scandal swept under the carpet, and Coutts Bank in control, the new town of Surbiton rapidly took shape. It was just the right distance from London to attract residents of a type never before seen in Kingston.

Surbiton Place was an important factor here. It was bought early in the 1850's by William Woods in a transaction that not only increased the importance of Surbiton as a new town, but brought the post-railway building boom close to the heart of Kingston for the first time.

The vivid story of this estate began in the mid-18th century when a wealthy distiller named William Roffee picked his ideal site to build a country seat. It was conveniently close to the rutted mud road to Ewell. It was near enough to the Thames to keep a fleet of pleasure boats. It was less than two miles from the centre of Kingston, yet enjoyed unbroken views in every direction. Here Mr Roffee gave parties of such magnificence that they were attended by Royalty and mentioned by Horace Walpole in one of his celebrated letters, dated 1773.

The estate was bought from Mr Roffee's executors by Thomas Fassett, who enlarged the house and grounds and, in the words of 19th century author G.F. Prosser, "indulged his predilection for al fresco amusements by the frequent assemblage of rural parties on this delightful spot."

Fassett eventually sold Surbiton Place to the 1st Earl of Uxbridge. He had been an impoverished nobody called Henry Bayly who, by a tortuous line of descent, unexpectedly became 9th Baron Paget and the owner of immense wealth. He had more good fortune in 1784 when the Earldom of Uxbridge, which had been created for the 7th Lord Paget and had died out with the eighth, was revived for the ninth.

His only ill luck was his face, described in a couplet by Peter Pinder:

"And he who lours as if he meant to bite
Is Earl of Uxbridge with his face of night."

This fearsome face belied his character, which was indolent, pleasure-loving and negative. He spent huge sums on Surbiton Place, where several of his 12 children were born, and where his pleasure was to have the band of the Staffordshire Militia, of which he was colonel, play on the terrace.

After his death in 1812, Surbiton Place passed to his son, Henry Paget, who became 1st Marquis of Anglesey in 1815 and has been immortalised for his gallantry as second-in-command to the Duke of Wellington at the Battle of Waterloo.

The French had been routed, and he was riding off the field with Wellington, when his right leg was shattered by grapeshot.

"By God, sir, I've lost my leg," he remarked, glancing down at the mangled stump. The Duke momentarily lowered the telescope through which he was watching the fleeing enemy. "By God, sir, so you have," he said. Then he resumed his telescope.

This famous tale is usually told as a classic example of gallant British cool. In fact, the coolness between the two men was due to a scandal which, in its effect upon the relationship between Paget, the greatest cavalry leader of the day, and Wellington, the greatest military commander, left its mark on history and on the name of a Surbiton road.

In 1795 Paget had married Lady Caroline Villiers, known as "Car." In 1803 Henry Wellesley, brother of the Duke of Wellington, had married Charlotte Sloane, daughter of the 1st Earl Cadogan, and always known as "Char."

In 1808 Char and Paget fell so violently in love that they eventually eloped, leaving Car with eight children and Henry Wellesley with four. The scandal enthralled the nation. Char's brother, Cadogan, challenged Paget to a duel on Wimbledon Common, but it ended in confusion. Henry Wellesley sued Paget for "criminal conversation" and was awarded a vast £20,000 in damages before obtaining a divorce by Act of Parliament in 1810. Car, by perjury and connivance, got her marriage dissolved in Scotland, English law at that time not allowing a wife to divorce her husband for adultery. Paget and Char then married and lived happily ever after, producing a further 10 children in the process.

> "My Lady and I have just calculated that she has cost me £20,000 for the first divorce, £10,000 for the second and £1,000 a year for Her Grace (Car) – and I must admit that I find her (Char) a good and cheap bargain notwithstanding," wrote Paget to his brother in 1811.

There is little doubt that Wellington despised Paget for ruining his brother's family life, and thereafter there was always some constraint between them.

Anglesey (he had been created Marquis within weeks of Waterloo) died in 1854, just as William Woods was laying out much of his former lands at Surbiton for housing. It explains why Woods named two of his new thoroughfares Uxbridge and Anglesea (sic). He must, however, have had tongue in cheek when he chose the name for Cadogan Road; for it commemorates Anglesey's liaison with Char, and there is a certain satire in naming such a sedate residential stronghold for a woman described by the Paget family as "a stinking polecat" and "the most wicked profligate whore and liar that ever hell itself could or ever will produce."

After the death of his mother in 1817, Anglesey sold the Surbiton Place estate. But his family was destined to renew its links with Kingston at the end of the century, when Pagets acquired the beautiful Warren House which, with its grounds, is still one of the glories of Kingston.

The next occupant of Surbiton Place was John Garratt, a member of Kingston Corporation and an alderman of the City of London, who laid the foundation stone of the new London Bridge in 1825 when he was Lord Mayor of London. He subsequently sold Surbiton Place to a wealthy individualist named Alexander Raphael, former MP for St Alban's and the first Roman Catholic to become Sheriff of London after the Catholic Emancipation Act.

Kingston knew him only as an eccentric recluse, whose sole public appearances were when he made a daily drive around the outer walls of his estate. Such aloofness was not surprising in a town long noted for its anti-Catholic feeling. As late as 1900, for example, the Revd Charles Stirling was writing to his former parishioners at New Malden apropos the Boer War: "The news from South Africa is indeed appalling but Romish priests of the idolatrous mass are found in the British camp and disaster must be expected." It was a view shared by many in Kingston.

Alexander Raphael has entered local legend because of an extraordinary story which he told his medical adviser, Dr Roots, who in turn recounted it to several Kingston townsmen. It was told again in the *Surrey Comet Diamond Jubilee* issue of June 1897.

It appears that during the 1840's, Mr Raphael became gravely ill. He recovered, against all the odds, and Dr Roots promptly presented his account, remarking that it was a heavy one because the illness had been so long. Mr Raphael retorted that his recovery was no thanks to the doctor, but to the fact that he had vowed to the Virgin Mary that if she would intercede for his recovery, he would build a church at a cost of £7,000. The result was the beautiful little St Raphael's Church, which he built on his estate at a time when there was no other Roman Catholic church in Kingston. However, Mr Raphael never worshipped there. He continued to attend Mass at Richmond. The reason is explained in the Diamond Jubilee booklet of St Raphael's Church, written by the Revd Peter Ryan in 1925 from authentic records. He describes how St Raphael's was begun in 1846, completed in 1848 and due to be consecrated that same year. However, Mr Raphael had a dream which foretold his death soon after the consecration. Predictably, he decided to defer the ceremony as long as possible. Several apointments were made with Bishop Nicholas Wiseman, head of what was then known as the London District. Each time they were cancelled. This continued until 1850 when, once again, arrangements were made for the consecration. This time Mr Raphael, through some oversight, did not revoke them. Bishop Wiseman, who later became the first Cardinal Archbishop of Westminster, arrived on the appointed day with his secretary and chaplain, Monsignor Francis Searle. He found the church locked and Mr Raphael away from home. However, the butler produced the key and the Bishop went ahead with the ceremony, accompanied only by Monsignor Searle. Mr Raphael was aghast when he found what had happened. He sacked the butler and within a few months he was dead, just as his dream had foretold. Now his remains lie in a handsome brass-studded coffin beneath the High Altar of the church he never used.

His memorial tablet, written in Latin above the West door, indicates he was far more than the recluse Kingston believed him to be. A translated extract reads: "Among the heated opinions of his time, he held an unswerving faith. He won for himself no small reputaion as a man of most refined culture, versed in many languages, most generous to the poor, of deep integrity to all. He gave much money to assist youth in need and to bring honour to the Catholic religion, not only in England but also in Italy and Germany. Because of his great merits, he was decorated by the Supreme Pontiff Pius IX with the honour and title of the Golden Knighthood of the Order of St Sylvester. He died 17th November 1850 aged 75. This monument to his piety was placed here by his sorrowing brother, sister and nephews."

The year of Raphael's death was also the year the Pope decreed that Bishop Wiseman should become the first Archbishop of Westminster. Mr Gower, a curate at All Saints, Kingston, inflamed the Royal Borough with a sermon in which he condemned the Pope's "usurpation of authority in this realm." William Drewett, in the Surrey Comet of November 5, 1924 recalled how enraged parishioners made an effigy of the new cardinal and carried it round the streets of Kingston before burning it on the Fairfield.

Surbiton Place passed to Alexander Raphael's nephew, Edward Raphael, who sold most of it to William Woods for housing development. However, the mansion itself was retained. Though left with only three of its former glorious acres, it was maintained in style under the new name Surbiton Hall by Mr John Shrubsole, owner of the banking and drapery business in Kingston Market Place which has evolved today into a branch of the National Westminster Bank and the Army and Navy store respectively. Mrs John Shrubsole spent her 40 years of widowhood there. King George V, Queen Mary and the Pre-Raphaelite painters Millais and Holman Hunt frequently visited her there and when she died in 1914 she left much of her jewellery to the Queen.

During its last years the mansion was the home of Sir Sidney Pocock. When he died in 1931 the old house died with him. Its contents were sold and almost at once it was demolished to make way for the houses that now stretch from 82 to 100 Surbiton Road, around the corner into Maple Road, and in Surbiton Hall Close.

The only other memorials to the estate are the names of the roads built by Woods across the once-noble park. They are, as we have seen, the Uxbridge, Anglesea and Cadogan Roads, together with Palace Road (so called because it is in direct line with Hampton Court Palace across the river), Surbiton Crescent and Grove Road. (Cleveland Road is named after a substantial 19th century developer, Cleveland Phillips.)

The last descriptions of Surbiton Hall are contained in the sale advertisements issued by auctioneers and estate agents Nightingale, Page and Bennett during June 1931:

> ". . . property of character and charm, most substantially built of brick with stone facings and slate roof, and presenting, with its creeper-clad walls and castellated parapets, a dwelling of considerable distinction, with lovely old-world gardens and 2¾ acres and nearly 700 ft of road frontage."

The advertisement lists accommodation of four reception rooms, billiard rooms, dressing rooms, 15 bedrooms and gardener's cottage.

Some idea of what Surbiton Place looked like at the height of its glory is contained in G.F. Prosser's *Select Illustrations of the County of Surrey*, published in 1828:

> "Principal entrance is by a vestibule, or Gothic porch, opening into a conservatory.
>
> "On each side a choice collection of aromatic plants is tastefully arranged. Folding glass doors are richly painted on the panes, and windows are set with tinted glass. The south

front presents at all seasons of the year a coup d'oeil of refreshing and perennial verdure, enriched by an extensive and beautiful lawn which is bounded by a lofty fence of evergreens. Among these several magnificent cedars, with the stately fir and ever verdant ilex, rear their heads in proud pre-eminence above the rest towards the view of Hampton Court Palace facade. Westwards is a neat dairy, with windows of painted glass, and beyond the handsome terrace overlooking the Thames are several cedars of striking magnificence. At one end is an elegantly constructed summer house . . . underneath is a grotto, formed with shells, and at the other is a capital boathouse, communicating with the river. On the other side of the road leading to Ewell are the extensive kitchen gardens, appropriate green and hothouses, peachery, grapery etc. with the coach house and stables adjoining."

Close to Surbiton Hall was another old estate whose acres were pared away over the years for building development. This was Elmers, a very old farm property which, before the Dissolution by Henry VIII, had belonged to the Charterhouse of London. It was granted to Kingston Corporation by Queen Elizabeth's second Grammar School charter, and was described then as "a messuage and barn in Surbiton, with 80 acres of land in the common fields." Until the 17th century it was called Beale's Farm. By the 19th century it had become a gentlemen's residence.

Its last occupant was Miss Frederica Rushbrooke, described in her obituary of October 21, 1882 as "a liberal subscriber to charity", who died while visiting her family's seat of Rushbrooke, near Bury St Edmunds. At her death Elmers had only 3½ acres left. Ten years previously, when 15 acres were acquired by the builders Corbett and McClymont of West Brompton for "the erection of houses that will bring many very wealthy families into the neighbourhood", it was stated that Miss Rushbrooke paid as much for the house and its remaining fragment of land as the whole estate had fetched but a short time previously.

The Elmers itself, described in the sale advertisements of 1883 as "a fine old gothic house of the 17th century" was eventually demolished to make way for Surbiton Assembly Rooms, which opened in 1889. Avenue Elmers and Claremont Gardens occupy part of its former grounds.

The Cranes was originally a 52-acre estate owned by the prominent local Jemmett family. It was auctioned off in May 1885 and Cranes Park and Cranes Park Avenue cut through the grounds, leaving The Cranes in a triangle formed by these two new roads and Villiers Avenue. By

1914 the house had disappeared to make way for Cranes Park Road and Cranes Park Crescent.

Hillcroft College in South Bank must be one of the best-preserved mansions of its kind left in Britain. Looking at its ornate pinnacles, gables, stained glass windows and Italian chimneys it is hard to credit that, figuratively speaking, it was built entirely from matchsticks.

The history of the building has its origins in 1836, when a Plymouth inventor named William Bryant joined business forces with a London grocer called Francis May. They became one of the world's first safety match manufacturers, and when William Bryant died in 1874 he was able to pass on a reasonably successful business to his four sons. The eldest, Wilberforce Bryant, then masterminded a great gamble. At that time foreign matches had a substantial portion of the British market and Wilberforce realised that his family's firm must have more efficient machinery if they were to compete successfully. He was a deeply religious man, and offered up heartfelt prayers after investing most of his resources in some 300 of the latest and best machines.

His prayers were answered. The new equipment enabled the factory in London's East End to produce close on two million boxes of matches a day, and soon Bryant and May were the most famous match manufacturers in the world, a distinction they can probably still claim today.

Wilberforce decided to celebrate his new fortune by building himself a mansion in Surbiton. He bought a large house in South Bank, had it demolished, and in 1877 built in its place the splendid residence that is now Hillcroft College.

He found life in Surbiton so much to his taste that by 1880 his brother, Arthur, had also made his home there. He settled at Oak Hill Lodge in Oak Hill Grove.

The Christian, strictly teetotal, Bryants had considerable impact on life in Surbiton and Kingston. Wilberforce believed that drink was the ruin of working men, and he set about organising "coffee taverns," where men could find the fellowship of a pub without the alcohol. His establishments included The Spread Eagle in Brighton Road and The Anchor in Ewell Road. He spent large sums equipping both places so customers could enjoy hot baths, freshly cooked meals and other comforts.

In 1884 Wilberforce Bryant set aside part of his estate to build a private meeting room and theatre. He called it The Gables because of its multi-gabled facade, and announced that "any useful or religious body" could use it free of charge. The Gables theatre eventually became more famous than the mansion in whose grounds it stood. During the Boer

War the then owner of the estate, Sir Alfred Cooper, liaised with Princess (later Queen) Alexandra to convert the building into the only private military hospital in the land. Wounded troops were brought ashore from the Princess of Wales' hospital ship at Southampton and brought straight to the Gables by the London and South Western Railway's ambulance coaches.

After the war, when the estate was bought by Mr Herbert Boret, The Gables reverted to its original purpose as a meeting place and theatre. It continued thus until 1935, when Hillcroft College, who had bought the estate in 1926, sold the theatre for re-development as the flats we know today as Glenbuck Court.

Meanwhile the Bryant brothers' two mansions still stand as part of Surbiton's rapidly dwindling heritage. Oak Hill Lodge, after years as a hotel and flats, is now a set of prestige offices known as The Sanctuary.

Hillcroft College (founded in Beckenham in 1920 to provide further education for women of limited education) has preserved Wilberforce Bryant's home in all its fine original detail.

Of all Surbiton's lively 19th century personalities, one of the most colourful was Daniel Nicols. He had been born Daniel Nicolas Thevenon, a native of Burgundy; but it was as Daniel Nicols, a naturalised Englishman, that he left Surbiton for the last time on March 4, 1897 in a splendid coffin of silver and mahogany, borne on a coach drawn by black-plumed horses and flanked by six outriders. Behind again came a long procession of mourners winding their way through the dense crowds who had come to pay their last respects. It was, as the *Kingston and Surbiton News* reported, a suitably stylish exit for the man who had revolutionised cafe society in Victorian London.

Thevenon had arrived in London in 1863 as a penniless wine merchant fleeing from his creditors and the French law. With him was his shy young wife, Celestine, who supported them in the first few months by taking in sewing. Their penury did not last long. Daniel was a man of great vision and energy and within two years he had changed his name to Nicols and opened modest refreshment rooms at 68 Regent Street. He called it the Café Restaurant Daniel Nicols, but soon it was attracting the best names in intellectual and political society, and he re-named it the Café Royal.

The Nicols wanted a country estate in keeping with their new wealth, and they chose it in Surbiton. Early in the 1870's they bought a large expanse of greenland formerly belonging to Berrylands Farm and on it built Regent House, a sumptuous mansion boasting the gaudy, almost decadent, opulence that was the hallmark of the Café Royal.

They engaged an Italian artist to cover the walls and ceilings with paintings and masses of gilding. Outside, Regent House was surrounded by 20 acres of ornamental gardens. Beyond that was a finely wooded deer park and Regent Farm. The whole estate comprised more than 100 acres, stretching from Berrylands to a point beyond the railway line.

Here Daniel and Celestine entertained on a tide of Pink Cliquot champagne. The ballroom at Regent House was huge, quite large enough to accommodate a full-size orchestra and the entire corps de ballet of the Empire Theatre who, with many music hall stars, came to amuse the weekend house parties.

It was easy for the Nicols to arrange such programmes, for in 1884 Daniel had taken over a derelict, half-completed building in central London and transformed it into the Empire Theatre. He intended it to be only a sideline, but it proved to have as big an impact as the Café Royal. From the start, the great crimson and gilt theatre, with its golden foyer, was the most luxurious ever seen in London, while from 1887 onwards – after three disastrous years of comic opera – it was noted as the first variety theatre in the world.

It was the improverished people of Surbiton who grieved most when Daniel died from diabetes, aged 67. Memories of his own early money troubles had made him generous to a fault and, to quote the *Kingston and Surbiton News* of March 6, 1897, "he was a good friend to the poor of the neighbourhood and no appeal was ever made to him in vain."

Daniel left more than £1m in a will which led to litigation of such proportions that it was taken to the House of Lords. His widow died in 1916 at the age of 85. To the end she continued to supervise the running of the Café Royal, spending the greater part of each week there and returning to Surbiton at weekends.

Today, the estate where Adelina Patti and other famous names made merry beneath canopies of naked nymphs is covered by the more modest residences of Park Road, Seymour Gardens, Regent Road, The Ridings, The Ridge, The Roystons and others. However, there are still reminders of its champagne past. One is Regent Cottage, the beautiful little building at 19 Berrylands that was once a coach-house on the Nicols' estate. The other is 69 Berrylands Road, one of the former lodges.

Incidentally, while Daniel Nicols was larger than life in his ideas, his son-in-law, George Pigache, was certainly that in his girth. After marrying the Nicols' only daughter, he became supervisor of the Café Royal kitchens. It was an occupation that made him so obese that, according to the *Café Royal, Ninety Years of Bohemia*, written by Guy Deghy and Keith Waterhouse in 1955, he was unable to get into the family coach for the morning drive to Surbiton Station. Instead he had to order a special cart from a local stable. Once at the station he could not get into the train without the help of three especially hefty porters, who were instructed to heave him into his railway carriage in the morning and painfully extract him from it at night. Pigache was only 47 when he died on May 13, 1898. The *Kingston and Surbiton News* of May 14 recorded that he weighed 36 stone, a fact which necessitated the removal of the banisters before the body could be brought downstairs.

Pigache, a noted wine connoisseur and amateur musician, lived and died at Vine House, which survived as 8 Park Road until 1970. Then it was demolished to make way for Vine Close.

Two of Britain's best-known novelists lived in 19th century Surbiton, Thomas Hardy began his married life in St David's Villa, Hook Road. It was cheap furnished accommodation, found by local estate agents Townly and Boniwell, where Hardy and his bride, Emma Gifford, arrived in 1875 with all their possessions in four boxes. During their sojourn there, Far from the Madding Crowd was published, and Hardy's fame and fortune steadily increased.

Some 30 years previously, William Thackeray had written his famous Vanity Fair while living in rooms in Surbiton. It was first brought out as monthly magazine instalments during 1847/48. Artist Holman Hunt in his, *Pre-Raphaelitism,* written in the 1880's and published in 1905, describes how he went to Surbiton to look for Thackeray after leaving a party at Hampton Court.

> "We arrived at the dark village and there was one house with a light on the first floor. It was easy to conclude we were at the right one and we all shouted out: 'Thackeray'. The window was forthwith opened and our friend appeared."

In 1853 Kingston Corporation introduced a Bill into Parliament to bring Surbiton within its borough boundaries. Surbiton vehemently opposed the move, objecting that their rates were being spent on Kingston while they were left "in barren dreariness, without gas or even the scavenger's besom." Their protests were so strong that, after two abortive appeals, Kingston lost the day and Surbiton obtained a bill to manage its own affairs under the Surbiton Improvement Commissioners.

The irony was that the very men fighting for Surbiton's independence were former Kingstonians like Samuel Ranyard who, some 15 years earlier, had fought all moves to develop and improve Surbiton and had contributed substantially to the downfall of the Pooleys.

Kingston Corporation was no model of efficiency or vision. Neither, in many ways, was the Surbiton Improvement Commission. For its first seven years, its meetings were devoted almost exclusively to the subject of drainage. Appropriately, these meetings were held above a stable in Victoria Road, in a room reeking with ordure. Finally in 1862, and after argument and counter argument, it was decided to adopt a plan by Robert Brown whereby the drainage passed to the Lambeth Waterworks sewer, with a tumbling bay in the middle of Surbiton Hill to speed it on its way.

Certainly the new commissioners had much to contend with. Mr Coleman, their medical officer, presented his report in March 1856 of conditions in the vicinity of Portsmouth Road. In George Street (now Cottage Grove) he found residents used the road as "an open sewer and general cesspool, throwing every kind of rubbish, liquid and solid, into it." Two hundred and fifty-two residents shared 40 four-roomed cottages – some with as many as 13 occupants. All the privies were at the end of the gardens, and the well that supplied the cottages with drinking water had a cesspool flowing into it.

In Westfield Road Mr Coleman found 263 people living in 42 houses, and noted that "residents have the objectionable habit of throwing house slops into the road." The houses, constructed only two years previously, had no drainage and the pump water was so filthy it was unfit even for washing. Water was laid from Lambeth Works, but because of the intermittent supply and the landlords not providing any cisterns, it was insufficient. It was turned on for only two-and-a-half hours each afternoon and not at all on Sundays. In Portsmouth Road, Mr Coleman found households had no water at all beyond what they fetched themselves from the Waggon and Horses pub.

As in Kingston, smell was a sickening problem. As Mr Coleman pointed out, all the open ditches of Surbiton were polluted by sewage which was taken a certain distance in pipes or drains before terminating in the ditches. The stench from these was carried by the wind to all parts of the area. Alpha Road was particularly bad, not only from the primitive drains but from the human ordure plentifully used in gardening. Britannia Road was described as "like a ploughed field" with the cellars of the Castle pub often four inches deep in water and the privies of the houses so full that their contents regurgitated into the wash-houses. He found the cottages in Ewell Road "abominable" with the ground "saturated with house slops" and "the contents of the privies welling through the ground into a potato garden."

Pigs formed a sizeable part of the population in the Queen of the

Suburbs. A letter in the *Surrey Comet* of November 10, 1855 pinpointed a nuisance that continued for most of the century.

> "Almost every man who rents a residence having a few feet of garden knocks up a sty and, commencing with one pig, soon has a litter; and not only a litter of pigs but a litter of garbage, filth and uncleanliness, with stenches execrable and nauseating stimulants inseparable from the conglomeration of the pig sties . . . men hawk their pork about to the injury of the butchers."

Eleven years later Mr Coleman, the medical officer, was complaining that one of his neighbours was keeping 17 pigs.

Slowly conditions improved, reaching a high point when Surbiton was lauded as Queen of the Suburbs because of the wealth of many of its residents and the splendour of their homes and roads. Much of this splendour survives today. Despite the ravages of the 20th century, Surbiton still defiantly retains an aura of sophistication and elegance far removed from its television joke image. Nevertheless, its queenly reign seems to have been brief, starting in the middle of the 19th century and ending at the start of the 20th. Its comeliness continued, but the rich, for the most part, sought pastures new.

"For years one rarely saw a board marked This House to Let. Now the wealthy people have gone further afield and Surbiton will never have the same class of residents again, while the value of house property in the district has diminished enormously," mourned Archdeacon Charles Burney in the *Diamond Jubilee Surrey Comet* of May 1897. He had been Vicar of St Mark's since 1870 and had a foot in every door.

Certainly by 1882, when railways were an established fact rather than a thrilling novelty, there was no longer the rush from what the estate agents termed "capitalists, noblemen, gentlemen, bankers and others" to snap up the Surbiton mansions. In June 1882 Surbiton Improvement Commission was dismayed to learn that there were many vacant houses and that £278 had been written off the rates during the past year compared with £255 the year before. Nevertheless, from a population of less than 200 in 1831 Surbiton had reached 7,642 in 1871. By 1881 that had risen to 9,416 residents living in 1,622 houses occupying 1,000 acres.

One reason for the noblemen's exodus may have been Surbiton's lack of public amenities. There was no library, no museum and the main lecture and entertainment hall was a redundant chapel in Maple Road. As for the elegant Surbiton Assembly Rooms – there were 30 years of argument and procrastination before they were finally opened in 1889 on what had been the site of The Elmers mansion. Still, the lack of amenities kept Surbiton's rates enviably low. On July 14, 1883 the *Kingston and Surbiton News* published the annual average rate in Surbiton, Kingston, Wimbledon, Twickenham and Teddington over the three years between 1881 to 1883. Kingston's rate was £13. 6s. 8d., while that of Surbiton was only £9. 3s. – the lowest of all the towns listed.

A reason for this was the Improvement Commissioners' skill in getting so many of their improvements subsidised. Maple Road was transformed from a muddy country lane to the handsome road we know today by getting the water companies to do the work at the time they were building their new filter beds at Seething Wells in 1856. Their big mains had to be brought along Maple Lane, as it then was, and the Commissioners insisted that in so doing they should make up and widen the road. The drainage scheme of 1862 has been largely financed by Earl Lovelace, the Temperance Land Society and Mr William Walter. Beautiful Claremont Gardens were maintained by the residents through a voluntary, self-imposed rate. Lambert's Road was due to the largesse of two residents. Until 1861 there was no road linking Surbiton Hill with Clay Lane (now Villiers Avenue) The only access was a path through the garden of the Railway Tavern. The problem was solved when Mr Lambert, whose Lambert House stood on the north side of the new road, and Mr Farnell, on the south, each gave up land for a road. The result was the opening of Lambert's Road on October 12, 1861.

Where Surbiton did score was in the provision of a cottage hospital years before Kingston. The idea of such hospitals had first been suggested by a Mr Napper of Cranleigh in 1859. He pointed out that the dwellings of the poor were utterly unfit to cope with illness or accident, and the answer would be to have cottage hospitals in every town and village. Surbiton opened its first cottage hospital on the site of the present Post Office in Victoria Road in 1871. By the end of 1880 the ledgers showed that 388 cases had been treated there, many gravely ill, and only 28 had died. In 1881 a new site, costing £1,125, was acquired in St James's Road and a permanent hospital opened there in 1883. It remained there until 1932, when a new hospital was built on the former site of Hill House, at the top of Surbiton Hill.

But it was not only good hospital care that gave Surbiton its low death rate – reported in February 1881, for example, to be only 14.3 per thousand compared with 17.3 for Kingston and 20.6 for all England. Part of the reason can be found in Dr Beale Collins' annual report of 1894 as medical Officer of Health for Kingston. He says of Surbiton: "the houses are many of them very large and occupied by wealthy men . . .

their servants are chiefly the daughters of the Kingston artisans and often return to their homes when sick and likely to die."

Throughout the later half of the 19th century, the relationship between Kingston and Surbiton could be likened to civil war as each fought for what they considered to be their territorial rights.

In 1894 Kingston made a superhuman effort to annexe Ham, Surbiton and New Malden into its municipal territory by means of the Kingston Extension Bill. Before this Bill could be presented to the House of Commons, it had to have the sanction of the Local Government Board. The Board held an Inquiry in December 1894. In March, after three months' tension, Kingston learned the result: the Board totally rejected the proposal and Thomas Guilford, who had led Surbiton's counter-attack against the Bill, was dined and feted as "the Wellington in the battle against Kingston."

It was a disastrous decision for Kingston, which had spent £2,600 on its extension attempt. Why? The reasons are set out in the letter which Kingston's Town Clerk, Mr Harold Winser, despatched to the Local Government Board's HQ in Whitehall as soon as the results of the Inquiry were made known. In it he points out that, because of recent orders by Surrey County Council, each of the districts adjoining the borough of Kingston were to be made into urban districts that in area would far exceed the borough itself.

Ham, to the North, would expand from 147 acres to 1,800. On the East, New Malden would, by being made to include Old Malden and Coombe, swell to over 3,100 acres. Surbiton, to the south, would, by the inclusion with it of Southborough, Hook and part of Long Ditton, become an urban district of 2,800 acres. Meanwhile Kingston was forced to remain with a restricted area of only 1,114 acres.

As a flag was hoisted up St Mark's spire to signal Surbiton's great triumph, Councillor William Allard told a meeting of Kingston Council: "The amalgamation will assuredly come at some future time to a Corporation more fortunate than ourselves."

He was a prophet indeed. In 1965, with the re-organisation of local government in Greater London, Surbiton, New Malden and parts of Ham were among the territories amalgamated with Kingston to form the Royal Borough of Kingston upon Thames.

Kingston-on-(and off) Railway

Kingston has always been derided for saying no to the great new concept of railways in 1834. That was the year Parliament passed the Bill for the London to Southampton rail. It was also the year when, it is alleged, Kingston refused to allow the line through its midst and so threw away the benefit for a main line station in the centre of the town. The station was sited at Surbiton instead, and Kingston's succeeding generations have had to make do with an inferior branch line service ever since. The result, it is claimed, was the rise of Surbiton and the corresponding decline of Kingston.

Is this true? Certainly Kingston was against the original route proposed by the London and Southampton Railway Co. There was no local newspaper at the time, and the council minutes are missing, but we have confirmation from respected Victorian chroniclers such as Frederick Merryweather, William Biden and Rowley Richardson. But that route did not pass through the town centre and did not include a central station. The station that Kingston repudiated would have been close to the Waggon and Horses at the foot of Surbiton Hill, not far from the spot where the station of 'New Kingston' eventually opened. Initial post-railway development would therefore still have been centred on Surbiton, and the effects on Kingston's trade and industry would still have been the same.

These facts, mentioned in *Surrey Comet* editions between 1856 and 1870, emerge most clearly from statements during a four-day hearing before a House of Commons Committee in 1860, when Kingston and Hampton Wick were each battling for the terminus of the proposed new branch line from Twickenham.

The proceedings, reported in depth in the *Surrey Comet* of May 26, also indicate that the railway company made no great effort to negotiate with Kingston in 1834. Indeed, it was the opposition of Lord Cottenham rather than of Kingston that probably induced them to divert their route. As Rowley Richardson recounts in his *Surbiton, Thirty-two years of Local Self-Government 1855-1887*, the original promoters intended that after Wimbledon the line would keep to the level ground at the foot of Wimbledon Hill and Coombe Hill, skirting Kingston and going through Molesey and Walton to Weybridge. But Lord Cottenham was loth to have his estate at Wimbledon disturbed and joined Kingston in resistance. The company seems to have wasted no time in parleying. A pamphlet of 1834 on *The Advantages and Profits of the London and Southampton Railway* states the policy of avoiding land whose owners offered opposition.

"The line was therefore carried through a barren and desolate country, where the soil was so valueless that landowners were glad to get rid of it at any price," declares the pamphlet, adding that landowners in Hampshire, who possessed the barren ground, were all in favour of the line. Those in Surrey were not so enthusiastic.

Cutting through Surbiton Hill, which meant shifting 500,000 cubic yards of clay, was an expensive undertaking; but it was deemed more economic than treating with intransigent landowners like Lord Cottenham. As it was, the cost of land and compensation amounted to £4,000 for every mile of the completed track to Southampton, but that was substantially less than that paid per mile by the Great Western, the London and Brighton and other contemporary companies.

Thus the first Kingston Station, so-called, was placed deep in a cutting to the west of the present Ewell Road Bridge. It was little better than a hut.

"There has been no unnecessary expenses in architectural designs or decorations, the object aimed at having been utility and durability at the smallest possible cost," said the company, describing its stations in a report presented at the half-yearly meeting of shareholders in February, 1839. It was a policy that was to enrage passengers for the rest of the century.

The first section of the London to Southampton line was constructed by the great contractor, Thomas Brassey. It ran from the London terminus at Nine Elms to Woking Common, with intermediate stations at Wandsworth, Wimbledon, Kingston, Ditton Marsh, Walton and Weybridge. (Later Nine Elms was re-named Vauxhall, Wandsworth became Clapham and Ditton Marsh was changed to Esher.)

Brassey, who went on to complete the line to Southampton, and who is said by the Dictionary of National Biography to have had "enterprises in every corner of the globe," made his home in Surbiton. He settled in Maple Lodge, formerly the homestead to Maple Farm, which stood roughly where the Claremont Hall is today.

The Nine Elms to Woking portion of the line was opened on May 21, 1838 to coincide with Epsom Races. An advertisement in *The Times* of

May 29 proclaimed that extra trains for Epsom Races would be run "to a point on the railway south of Kingston which is nearest to Epsom." This advertisement had spectacular results. Reported *The Times* of May 31:

> "It is speaking very much within bounds to say that at an early hour upwards of 5,000 persons were assembled at the gates of the Southampton Railway near Vauxhall for the purpose of going by the railroad trains to Kingston Station, and from thence by other conveyances to the race course . . . hundreds were to be disappointed.
>
> "There were ten times more applicants for seats in the train vans than there were seats for their accommodation. The proprietors did what they could to meet the demands for conveyance, but they could not do what was impossible."

C.F. Dendy Marshall, in his *History of the Southern Railway*, quotes from a letter written by the London and Southampton Company's secretary to the editor of *Railway Magazine* shortly afterwards:

> "Although there are seven stopping places between London and Woking, the engines perform their journey of 23 miles within the hour. Among the engines, those made by Rennie and Co. have been particularly remarkable by the simplicity and excellence of construction and the ease and rapidity with which they perform the journey, often at the rate of between 40 and 50 mph."

The company's first timetable shows five trains daily each way on the new line, stopping at every station. Thirty-one minutes were allowed for the 10¼ miles between Nine Elms and Surbiton at a fare of 3s. for a first-class seat and 1s. 6d. for a second.

Frederick Merryweather has left a vivid description of those early trains in his *Half a Century of Kingston History*:

> "The first-class carriages were low and narrow inside; the luggage was strapped on the roof. The second-class were fitted with bare seats and with open, unsashed windows which made umbrellas requisite in rainy weather. The third-class ran but once a day, were purposely made as uncomfortable as possible, and were attached to a heavy goods train which shunted at almost every station; they were open trucks with the rudest of benches.
>
> "The guard's seat was on the roof of one of the carriages, from which he worked a primitive brake which consisted of a shaft or rod underneath the carriage, attached to the brake blocks, with a connecting rod running up to the guard's seat. The position was uncomfortable and hazardous. Night or day,

> through wind or storm, through tunnels and the bleakest country, smothered with smoke or blistered with sparks and dust, the poor guard was often so perished and benumbed as to be unable, when he reached the terminus, to leave his seat without help."

The diary of William Lucas of Hitchin, written between 1804 and 1861, and published in 1934 as *A Quaker Journal*, gives an interesting glimpse of how the London and Southampton Co's service compared with that of its bitter rival, the Great Western. On July 9, 1838 Lucas noted:

> "To Uxbridge by the Great Western Railway. Sad want of punctuality at starting, and when off rate at only 14 miles an hour. How have the mighty promises of Brunel fallen."

Four days later he wrote:

> "Went to the Kingston Station of the Southampton railroad, saw several trains, punctuality admirable, rate above 30 miles an hour, not many passengers."

The original crude little station, reached by a steep descent down the embankment from South Terrace, was so unattractive to passengers that in 1839 the Surbiton developer, Thomas Pooley, gave the company Surbiton Station's present site. Here was built what *The Times* described as "a very respectable edifice."

Even so, it was primitive in its signalling and passenger arrangements. William Drewett, in the *Surrey Comet* of May 23, 1925, recalled that the ticket office closed five minutes before the departure of each train. A handbell was rung to announce the arrival of a train as soon as its steam was seen on the horizon. To reach Ewell Road passengers passed through fields and gates and climbed a stile.

In those early days, before the advent of mechanised signals, railway personnel were given distinctive red neckerchiefs known as 'flamers'. These could be whipped off and waved as an emergency signal in times of danger. The *Kingston and Surbiton News,* recalling this in its issue of June 8, 1889, reported that 'flamers' were still worn by LSWR porters, and were about to be issued to shunters and yardmen. They were no longer needed as signals but were, said the company, valuable as bandages or tourniquets in case of accident!

In 1839 the London and Southampton Co. changed its name by Act of Parliament to the London and South Western Railway. The following year, the 77-mile line from London to Southampton was completed by Thomas Brassey and in 1848, following an extension to the line of one-and-three-quarter miles, the London terminus was moved from Nine Elms to Waterloo.

Standards on board the trains continued to be appalling for several years, as did the conduct of the 'noble' passengers from Surbiton, long the most profitable station on the line. The founder of the *Surrey Comet,* Thomas Philpott, wrote acidly in his newspaper during the 1850's of gentlemen in first-class carriages who not only ignored the No Smoking notices, but who used the carriages as 'locomotive spitoons'. When New Kingston's first railway inspector, Mr Dudman, reported this disgusting conduct to his directors, he was told to "mind his own business" – and to remember that fares in the first-class carriages were 15% higher than in the second!

Philpott also condemned conditions in the third-class accommodation, grudgingly provided only because Parliament had decreed that one train a day should provide third-class travel at a penny a mile.

"This train always left Waterloo at quarter past seven, but no sooner have the mornings become dark and cold than the directors alter the time to 6 a.m. so as to give the greatest amount of discomfort to the travellers," he said. However, following Government legislation in 1844, the LSWR had at least eased the sufferings of third-class travellers by replacing the former open trucks with three-compartment 'Parliamentay carriages' seating 30.

Filth was something all three classes had in common.

"Were the first-class carriages scraped, and the produce placed in that general receptacle known among the red-faced fairies of the cuisine as a grease pot, the result would produce a beaming smile, even at their hottest moment," declared the *Surrey Comet's* leader column of August 17, 1856.

Passengers who survived their train journey had to brave the brawls that were a frequent occurrence at New Kingston Station because of the fierce competition for customers among the various omnibus firms. A typical instance is described in the *Surrey Comet* of January 24, 1857:

> "On Monday afternoon a pugilistic encounter took place near the railway station between Faulkner, the driver of Messrs Williams and Linton's omnibus, and Richards, the conductor of the opposition vehicle belonging to Mr Marriott. The affray came out of the ill feeling that has for some time existed among the parties interested in the success of the competing conveyances, and was very particularly manifested on this occasion.
>
> "The vilest epithets were liberally supplied by both men, which resulted in a regular fight; and on Faulkner levelling his opponent to the ground, he unfortunately fell on him and

broke his leg in two places. The injured man remains in a very precarious condition."

(The 'Williams and Linton' referred to were John Williams and Joseph Linton, who were respectively propietor and carriage master of Kingston's Griffin Hotel, and ran an omnibus service between it and the station at Surbiton. Mr Marriott was a well-known omnibus proprietor.)

Bitter omnibus rivalry continued for the rest of the century, with constant Press reports of vehicles racing two and three abreast and literally trying to run each other off the road to the danger, and sometimes the injury, of passengers and pedestrians.

With the filth of the rail carriages and the dangerous tactics of the omnibuses, it is small wonder that the old-fashioned stage coach continued to attract passengers throughout the 19th century.

"Coaching will always have its charms so long as country roads and sweet-smelling hedgerows continue," remarked the *Surrey Comet's* leader column of May 27, 1882. "One tires of the monotony of railway travelling and the incidence of stuffy cushions and frowsy paddings of the first-class carriages in hot weather." It went on to extol the "well appointed coach". The Wonder, which the following week was to start a thrice-weekly service from Surbiton Station to Blackfriars, leaving at 9 a.m. and arriving at 10.45 a.m.

Earlier, on April 12, 1879, the *Surrey Comet's* leader column had evoked old memories of coaching:

> "Oh, what a joy it was to mount the box or scramble on the seat next to the guard. To hear the whip sharply crack and the shrill too-tooing of the horn rousing up a whole village as the coach rattled through, setting children screaming with delight, the dogs barking and the geese hissing angrily as they flew before the prancing leaders. What fun it was as we spun along all day long through roads redolent with the perfume of newly-made hay at the spanking rate of 10 mph."

The column commented on the number of stage coach services inaugurated since 1869, adding that the Box Hill coach still left The Swan at Thames Ditton each day for London, while a four-horse coach left The Griffin in Kingston for the White Horse cellars in London three days a week. Twenty years after the opening of the London to Southampton railway. The Age coach to Brighton was still stopping at the Kings Arms in Kingston and the Black Lion in Surbiton, while in 1880 Mr P.D. Rumney and a Surbiton syndicate launched the Early Times coach, which ran between London and Surbiton throughout the winter.

Perhaps the best-known of all these late 19th century coaching services was the New Times, launched by Mr Walter Schoolbred in 1874 and saluted by the *Kingston and Surbiton News* of May 2, 1896 as it started its 22nd season, travelling daily between Guildford and London with a stop in Kingston Market Place.

Two decades after the railway had reached Surbiton, Kingston was still without a town station of its own and, but for William Bull, it is doubtful if the LSWR would ever have provided one.

On October 2, 1858 the *Surrey Comet* published a letter from Mr Bull in which he detailed his design for a railway "to connect with the existing system of railways north and south of the Thames Valley by a line through Kingston, making Kingston the central station." His eight-and-a-half-mile line would run from Isleworth to Malden, via Richmond, Hampton Wick, Kingston and Norbiton, at a fare of a penny per mile. There would also be a junction line between the stations at Kingston and Surbiton, running along the west side of the Fairfield.

The LSWR, scenting serious competition, moved swiftly. By July 1859 it had applied to Parliament for a Bill to form "a short branch line from Twickenham to Kingston". In fact, the line was to terminate near the Hampton Wick side of Kingston Bridge, which was then still subject to tolls. Kingston felt that the LSWR was a safer option than William Bull, but was outraged at the prospect of having to pay a halfpenny bridge toll to reach the station.

The hapless Mr Bull became a pawn, Kingston threatening to throw in its lot with him unless the LSWR agreed to site its terminus in Kingston instead of Hampton Wick. Predictably, Hampton Wick was incensed that instead of its promised terminus, it would have to suffer the greater loss of land, property and peace involved in running a railway right through the village and over the river. It appealed to Parliament, but after a four-day hearing Kinston won, and Mr Bull had the dubious honour of seeing much of his scheme brought to fruition by his LSWR rivals.

Mr Bull had intended to bring a line to Kingston via a bridge over the Thames. That is what the LSWR did. He had planned to locate Kingston's first town station in Fitt's Market Gardens. The LSWR did exactly that. They also managed to oust Mr Bull for but a modest outlay. As their traffic manager, Archibald Scott, told the Parliamentary Committee, their trains could be moved from Twickenham to Kingston at very little expense.

Instead of blowing off their steam at Twickenham, they could go on a mere three-and-a-half miles to Kingston and do it there instead.

Kingston was not as desperate to acquire a station as is commonly thought. Many people wanted the terminus to remain on the Middlesex bank, and thousands petitioned aginst the line being brought over the Thames to Kingston.

"The small encouragement, or rather opposition, the London and South West Railway have uniformly met with at the hands of the majority of the townsfolk may render the directors inattentive to the real requirements of the district," warned the *Surrey Comet's* leader column of November 19, 1859.

Prominent among the protestors were John Guy, a wealthy solicitor living at Norbiton Hall; the three Misses Fisher of Canbury Lodge (later to become the site of Kingston bus garage) and the distinguished Dr Sudlow Roots of Canbury House (later the site of Kingston Empire). They feared that once the line reached Kingston, it would soon be extended to Norbiton and Malden and their peaceful estates, together with the whole north side of Kingston, would be permanently despoiled.

Archibald Scott ridiculed such prophecies. "There is no probability of a line being carried on to Malden by the LSWR or any other company," he told the inquiry.

A year later, on May 29, 1861, the first spade of earth for the new rail embankment on the Kingston side of the river was turned in what had been Goldring's garden in Lower Ham Road. The line was carried over the road on an arch before running through the extensive market gardens where the Fitt family had lately grown rich crops of salad vegetables for the London market.

In fact, until the arrival of the railway, market gardens extended south from Canbury Passage to Clarence Street, covering what is now the station approach of Wood Street and the whole of Fife Road. The station itself, with its attendant goods depot and engine sheds, was built on what had been the site of one of the largest tithe barns in Britain.

It took two years to construct the new line. It was a project that changed a part of the town beyond recognition and was clearly going to bring about even greater topographical and social changes in the future. Yet, incredibly, the exercise was scarcely mentioned in the local Press. Was this an indication of public indifference?

Those references that did appear were approving. The bridge, built to carry the rail across the Thames from Hampton Wick, was described by the *Surrey Comet* of May 16, 1863 as "not the eyesore that had been feared, but light and graceful". The station was said to be "far superior" to its counterpart at Surbiton and "a facsimile, on a small scale, of Waterloo Station".

The bridge was designed by John Errington, a distinguished railway engineer who had been involved in the construction of many lines throughout Britain. His bridge, constructed by Brassey and Co. and still surviving today, consists of five cast iron arches, each with a 75 foot clear span. Its "light and graceful" appearance was marred in 1889 when the LSWR gave permission for an iron sewage main to be attached to it so that Hampton Wick could send its sewage to the new Native Guano works in Down Hall meadows.

John Errington did not live to see completion of his bridge, or of the line, which was also his design. He died in July 1862 at the age of 56 and his project was finished by LSWR engineer, Mr Galbraith.

Kingston Station was designed by John Strapp, who had been an assistant to Thomas Brassey in the construction of the Nine Elms to Surbiton Line and became the LSWR's chief resident engineer in 1856. Like so many prominent railway pioneers, he settled in Surbiton, where he became an Improvement Commissioner and a churchwarden at St Mark's.

The line from Twickenham to Kingston opened on July 1, 1863 with only moderate attention from the local Press. The initial service offered 15 up and 13 down trains daily, travelling to and from Waterloo via Richmond. A further nine trains ran direct to Fenchurch Street in the City. Odious comparisons were soon made with Surbiton, who by then could boast more than 50 trains daily in each direction. Time was another factor. Passengers from Surbiton could get to Waterloo in 30 minutes or less. From Kingston the journey took more than an hour. Soon antipathy towards the LSWR was as marked at Kingston as it had been for the past quarter-century at Surbiton and Malden, as the company failed to fulfil earlier promises.

"Where are the cheap, fast trains?" demanded a correspondent in the *Surrey Comet* of February 2, 1864, adding that the cheapest fare to London from Kingston was two shillings at a speed little swifter than that of a stage coach. Croydon people, meanwhile, got to London for a shilling in 25 or 30 minutes – half the time and half the price!

Within two years of the Kingston Station opening, John Guy's prophecies came true. The LSWR, which had declared they would never extend the line, obtained powers so to do. In July 1865 the Kingston Further Extension Act authorised them to construct a line similar in route to that proposed by William Bull seven years previously.

It ran through Norbiton and passed under the Southampton main line at Malden, running parallel with its south side to Wimbledon. From there it ran direct to Ludgate Hill, passengers for Waterloo being obliged to change at Wimbledon. Further powers were obtained in 1866 to raise the line between Norbiton and Kingston so it could pass over the London and the Richmond Roads on arches, joining the existing line on Kingston's side of the Thames rail bridge.

This meant considerable alterations to John Strapp's attractive little low-level station terminal. It also meant the break-up of the Canbury Lodge Estate, the transformation of what had once been the rural Canbury Lane into the densely developed Richmond Road and the departure from Norbiton Hall of John Guy. Outraged at the prospect of a railway line going through the fields of Norbiton, he sold up.

One of the benefits of the new line, opened on January 1, 1869, was that it provided the developing area of Norbiton with rail facilities. Norbiton Station was built amid the fields on the south side of Coombe Road and survives today as the Royal Borough's sole remaining example of 19th century station architecture. The only major alteration to the original was the construction in 1884 of the subway that links the up and down platforms. Announcing this improvement in the *Kingston and Surbiton News* of January 26, 1884, the LSWR remarked that 26,000 passengers had used Norbiton Station in the past year.

There had been public animosity towards the LSWR ever since the opening of the station at Surbiton. This antipathy increased throughout the century.

"How this neighbourhood has suffered because the railway company is independent of any kind of public control," commented the *Kingston and Surbiton News* of June 8, 1881, reporting passengers' complaints of "unpunctuality, wretched and short carriage accommodation and patched-up stations."

The previous month the paper had reported how the town clerk, Mr Walter Wilkinson, had driven his mare from Kingston to London in one-and-a-half hours – considerably faster than he could get there by the LSWR – and at a public meeting held in Kingston in February 1881 to discuss the new Kingston and London Railway scheme, passengers complained how they had been forced to leave first-class carriages for second class ones because of "stinking cushions full of dirt".

News that the Kingston and London company were to build a new line was hailed with joy by Kingston in that it would at last break the monoply of the LSWR as well as vastly improving local rail amenities. The route the new rail was to take was described in detail in the *Surrey Comet* of January 8, 1881. Starting at Fulham, it would cross the Thames near Putney Bridge, approach Kingston close to Coombe Lane West, then pass through a field at the corner of Gloucester Road. From there it would cross Cambridge Road, continuing via Cambridge Grove, Washington Road and a route parellel with Clay Hill (now part of Villiers Road). After crossing the Surbiton line above Surbiton Station it would pass through the Southborough estate, touching Hook, and thence to Guildford via Cobham. The mile or so of line that would be within the Kingston borough boundary would pass over the town on arches 15 foot high and 25 foot wide. In May the Guildford, Kingston and London Rail Bill passed its second reading in the Commons. In April Kingston was enraged to learn that at the eleventh hour the promoters had planned an amalgamation with the LSWR.

There would be no independent line after all. The eventual outcome was that the LSWR opened the new Guildford line between Guildford and Surbiton on February 2, 1885 to link with their line at Hampton Court Junction.

The line from Kingston to Putney Bridge was to be built by a newly-formed company. However, in 1886 the LSWR managed to get this line diverted from its monopoly territory at Kingston. The result was the Wimbledon to Putney line, opened on June 3, 1889.

Kingston was left only with dashed hopes and some partially completed rail routes. These are still visible today, on territory to the north of Kingston By-Pass, as a reminder of what might have been.

The LSWR continued to rule supreme over Kingston until the Railway Act of 1921 merged all Britain's railways into four main groups. The LSWR was amalgamated with the London, Chatham and Dover to form the new Southern Railway, launched in January 1923.

In 1934 Kingston Station was rebuilt. Among the new developments was a large concourse with a subway to the up-platform. Today the only reminder of the old days is a remnant of the low-level station, raised and re-aligned to form a siding.

Surbiton's Victorian Station, largely re-constructed in 1883, was entirely replaced in 1938 with a building that has since been listed by the Department of the Environment as an outstanding architectural example of its type and period.

Home Sweet Home

The house-building boom that followed the opening of the station at Kingston-on-Railway was like a wave, engulfing acre after acre and changing the landscape beyond recognition. Certain vested interests regarded this tidal change with hostility and fear; but ordinary Kingstonians watched, enthralled, as one large villa succeeded another at the southernmost end of the parish. It became a family pastime to go sightseeing on the new estates taking shape on what had previously been farmland and untamed common.

This was the honeymoon of Kingston's post-railway building revolution. Soon it would sour, and public attitudes take a different turn; but there was no thought of that when two events occurred which brought that revolution, hitherto confined to the 'new' town of Surbiton, close to the centre of old Kingston.

The first was the death in 1850 of Alexander Raphael, who had lived as a semi-recluse in his mansion, Surbiton Place. After his death, most of his beautiful wooded acres were bought by an astute developer named William Woods. By 1855, Mr Woods had laid out Surbiton Crescent and the Uxbridge, Anglesea and Palace Roads across Mr Raphael's former secluded domain. He had also created Grove Road, embarked on a programme of 300 houses and constructed a part of the lovely riverside promenade.

The second event was Charles Rowlls' decision in 1854 to sell his Kingston Brewery and to lease much of his extensive lands in Kingston for building.

The brewery, as recalled in the *Kingston and Surbiton News* of April 29, 1889, had for many years been rated as the largest single-handed business of its kind in the London area. It occupied the west side of Brook Street and the Rowlls family, who had owned it since 1745, lived on the brewery estate in the fine 18th century mansion, Kingston Hall. The house was approached through a grove of elms and a pair of wrought-iron gates, situated at the point where St James's Road and

Eden Street now meet. Each day the gates would open for Madam Catherine Rowlls – she seems always to have been called 'madam' – to take the air in a stately carriage drawn by two black horses.

The pleasure grounds, known as Rowlls Park, included most of the land between the brewery and the back of High Street, stretching south as far as Oaklea Passage and the Bittoms.

"Kingston Hall stood in perfectly rural surrondings, though in the heart of the town, with a purling stream running through the grounds, and rooks innumerable cawing for all they were worth in due season," recalled the *Kingston and Surbiton News.*

This idyllic scene disappeared after the sale of the brewery to William Hodgson. Kingston Hall was demolished, the meandering Hogsmill stream was straightened, and in 1858 St James's Road was cut through Rowlls Park, with a stout brick bridge to carry it over the water and so provide a direct route to Surbiton and its all-important station.

Kingston exulted in these developments. Trade in the old town had been moribund even before the advent of the London and South Western Railway. As early as 1834, a Parliamentary Commission had described the local economy as 'stationary'. In the years following, the decline had become catastrophic as the new transport rapidly carried away trades that had been the backbone of local business. New roads and houses would bring new residents; and new residents, it was hoped, would breathe fresh life into dying trade.

The infant *Surrey Comet,* created by Thomas Philpott in 1854, rejoiced that, at last, Kingston was benefitting from the steam age.

> "Anyone who has been absent from the neighbourhood for the last year or two would scarcely recognise old associations or former haunts," he wrote in his leader column of September 15, 1855. "The extensive grounds of C. Rowlls Esq. are now being laid out for building purposes and ere long will prove ornamental and materially promote the trade of the town. Proceeding along the Portsmouth Road, it is a matter of positive astonishment to see the changes that have taken place, especially in the capacious park formerly belonging to the late A. Raphael Esq. and which, since that gentleman's death, has been devoted to far more practical uses than it was during the time he held possession of the property.
>
> "Roads have been formed and several first-class mansions and other elegant residences have been reared; and as the eye of the pedestrian wanders over the mighty improvements, he cannot fail to be struck with the beauty and adaptability of the site . . . on every hand we behold the wonderful

effects of art and science, aided by the appliance of mechanical skill, and the benefits that have resulted are felt to a considerable extent by tradesmen, especially of this neighbourhood. This district, which but a short time since in some parts was all but a sterile blank . . . bids fair to rank, at no distant time, as one of our most important surburban districts."

Thomas Philpott was adept at capturing the local mood of the moment. The success of his little paper depended on it. He was also a noted Christian, with a pious regard for the truth. So it can be assumed that his unbridled enthusiasm was an accurate reflection of public opinion.

In a town that had known only pumps, wells and open tanks, he was surely not alone in his joyful wonder at the great waterworks being constructed at Seething Wells, alongside the turnpike road to Portsmouth. The building of the Lambeth Works and reservoir began on a 30-acre site in 1849 and was completed in 1851. The following year, Chelsea Water Company began a similar undertaking on an adjoining site of 40 acres.

> "On taking a view of both these monuments of mechanical skill and manual labour, one cannot but be filled with astonishment and inhale an inspiration of grateful emotion that our species is so wonderfully endowed by a beneficient creator, not only with possessing the ability and inheriting the appliances ready to perfect and carry ideas of such magnitude, but to make them adaptable channels for ministering to the comforts and health of the population," wrote Philpott in the *Surrey Comet* of September 22, 1855.

By 1856, Philpott was noting "that the fields surrounding the town have become so densely crowded with houses that Norbiton and Surbiton far out number in population the original town."

By September 1859 the *Surrey Comet's* new owner and Editor, Russell Knapp, could announce that 3,500 new homes had been built in the neighbourhood. Early in the following year, in a memorial from Kingston to the London and South Western Railway, it was stated that the population of Kingston had nearly doubled since the opening of the station at Surbiton.

Building speculation became a fever, and in the rush for land none of Kingston's several farms and mansions remained intact. Many men of humble origin achieved wealth through shrewd land purchase and development. A typical example was James Goulter. He and his family appear in the 1841 Census as bricklayers; but he went on to develop much of the Kingston Hill estate, including the Alexandra, New and Tudor Roads. The Alexandra Hotel, which he built for himself in 1868, and which still flourishes in Park Road, was his proudest creation. Another success was James Boxall, who bought land all over Kingston when it was still cheap and plentiful in the '30's and '40's and built houses that increased phenomenally in value. Today his best-known building is Eagle Chambers, which he built in 1879 at the Market Place end of Eden Street.

Others, as a look at the bankruptcy lists of the period will show, were not so shrewd. On January 24, 1857, the *Surrey Comet* was lamenting "reckless speculators, who begin apparently large undertakings, collect a large number of workers then, not having counted the cost, come to a dead stop and throw all the unfortunate men out of employment." By July 15, 1865, the paper was stating that so great was the number of bankruptcies in Kingston that some firms were refusing to deal with local businessmen until ready money had been given.

After the opening of Kingston Station in 1863, working class accommodation became scarcer and rents higher as the population increased. Cottages that had formerly let at 3s. 6d. to 4s. 6d. per week had increased in rent to between 6s. 6d. and 7s. 6d. – a sum beyond the means of many working men. For most of the second half of the 19th century, the living conditions of Kingston's artisans were appalling. The creation of railway extensions, new sewers and many new roads and houses, coupled with the birth of new industries in Kingston, required the services of a substantial labouring population. Yet little thought had been given to providing them with suitable homes.

The *Surrey Comet* summed up the situation in its leader column of May 27, 1865:

> "There is nothing more agreeble to owners of land and houses, and all engaged in business in the neighbourhood of Kingston, than to notice the numerous beautiful and commodious residences rapidly covering the ground and inhabited as soon as finished. To the first it tells of increased value of land and high rents. To the second it indicates the influx of numerous families of good means, the supply of whose wants must greatly stimulate the trade of the town . . . but there is a reverse side of the medal which is not so pleasant to look at. To the numbers who live in humble habitations, the almost exclusive building of high-rated houses in Kingston is attended by serious ills. The influx of well-to-do families, living in a state of refined comfort, if not of positive luxury, has caused a corresponding increase of the class engaged in

ministering to their wants in various industrial occupations . . . and as they must live near their employment, a greatly increased demand for cottages has arisen. But there is no corresponding increase of supply. Small houses are bespoke before they are finished and landlords have applicants by the score whenever a vacancy occurs. Rents are now nearly double what a working man can afford to pay. Recently we mentioned an instance where the tenants of 30 cottages received simultaneous notice that their rents would be raised from 5s. 9d. to 7s. 9d. a week, and if they did not pay, they must leave in a week. And these cottages contain but four rooms . . . Rent ought not to be more than a fifth of a man's income. A man earning 25s. to 30s. a week should not stake more than 4s. 6d. to 6s. a week in rent."

Many earned far less than that. A study of local newspapers shows that pay could be as low as 12s. a week and 24s. was common for most of the century.

To meet rent bills, tenants had to take in lodgers. The result was that overcrowding in Kingston became worse each year.

"The family that ought to have four rooms as a minimum for health and decency frequently has to make do with only two, and a sheet hung up is often the only division between the sleeping places of adults of both sexes. Sometimes as many as seven or eight lodgers share a tiny house with a family," declared Russell Knapp.

"Single men herd together in small apartments . . . they rise languid and dull instead of refreshed and active. We are writing now of the better class working men. There are classes below them in the social scale whose condition is very much worse, and whose moral state may be judged by anyone who chooses to attend when any of the very frequent summonses between neighbours for abusive words are being heard by the magistrates. He will there be amazed that the vocabulary of the alehouse is as perfectly understood by many of the ladies in the Back Lanes of Kingston as by any fish fag in Billingsgate."

It was a social problem sadly prevalent throughout England, as shown by the Royal Commission on Housing in 1885.

Knapp, as an astute businessman, realised that the big capitalists were not generally interested in building workmen's cottages. He and his more enlightened readers called repeatedly for "a combination of small men. A limited liability company expressly for building respectable cottages for the working classes, and also small villas for the middling classes"; for rents of these, too, had increased substantially. Houses that had formerly let at £15 to £20 a year were now £25 to £30, yet were too small to accommodate a family and a servant.

As a reader pointed out in a letter published on June 3, 1865: "When we think that the new railway line will bring numbers of clerks and office men to the neighbourhood, if suitable residences are to be found, it behoves those who wish to see the north of Kingston, especially, equally flourishing with the south to put their shoulder to the wheel as proof that no time must be lost."

The problem was made worse by the demolition of houses to make way for the new extension line from Kingston to Malden, opened on January 1, 1869. This same reader commented that the occupiers of almost every house in Norbiton "between the Post Office and the Black Horse" had had notice to quit because the land was needed for the new railway. All were highly respectable working people who would be a great loss to the neighbourhood.

It was to be another 30 years before Kingston built its first council houses for working people, and squalid living conditions continued to be an increasing blot on the town's landscape for the rest of the century.

Nevertheless, the *Surrey Comet's* persistent campaigning did much to prompt the formation of the Kingston Building Society, formed on June 14, 1865 in St Peter's schoolroom in Hawks Road. The first trustees were John Collings, together with Benjamin Looker, a local brick-maker, and James Goulter, a builder. Mr Collings took the chair and delivered some plain speaking. No-one, he said, was going to provide cottages as a charity. Working people must combine, and by their united subscriptions achieve homes for themselves.

The society progressed modestly. There were 79 members in the first year, total receipts were £303. 3s. and £50 was advanced on mortgage. But by 1931, when the Society opened new headquarters in Eden Street, it had enabled more than 6,000 people to become house owners.

The Starr Bowkett Building Society established a Kingston branch in November, 1865. This Society had been founded by a Mr Bowkett, and subsequently improved by a Mr Starr. In fact, it was Mr Starr himself who launched the Kingston branch, explaining at a public lecture how one could build a £300 house for 1s. 3d. per week and a £250 house for 1s. per week. This, at a time when a four-roomed cottage cost £120 to build and up to 7s. 6d. a week to rent, was an enticing prospect. Hundreds of working men seized the opportunity to become owner-occupiers. Soon Kingston had four branches of the Starr Bowkett Society.

Land societies had been introduced some 20 years previously. An early example was the national Freehold Land Society, founded in 1849. Four years later it had amassed more than £¼m, and was using part of its funds to buy acres on the undeveloped slopes of Kingston Hill. The story of how the site was transformed into a genteel residential estate is told by G.N. Gandy in his *Life of a Victorian Suburb*, published in 1966 in volume 63 of the Surrey Archaelogical Collections. By 1854 the Society (which evolved into today's Abbey National) had constructed the Tudor, Queen's, Liverpool and Crescent Roads and begun selling plots to shareholders; but it took more than 50 years to cover the land with houses, probably because of building difficulties caused by the many underground springs in the area.

Another similar body was the Conservative Land Society, formed in 1851. During the 1870's it bought Kingston's old Militia Barracks and subsequently sold the site as building plots with frontages to the Fairfield and the newly-constructed Ashdown Road, named in memory of the Society's late secretary.

A Conservative Land Society advertisement in the *Surrey Comet* of November 15, 1856 describes the modus operandi:

> "By paying 8s. per month, and another 1s. quarterly, any person (children as well as ladies) may become the holder of a £50 share without partnership liability of any kind. The entrance fee per share 2s. 6d., and a pass book (for any number of shares) costs 1s. The first enrolment would therefore be 19s. 6d. and 8s. monthly afterwards. Sums of £5 and upwards bear interest at the rate of 5% per annum, paid half-yearly . . . all members, whether they pay their subscriptions monthly in advance or take completed shares, price £52 4s. 6d. each, participate in the annual division of the profits. The taking of land is quite optional."

Originally the prime aim of the land societies had been to enable the lower classes to acquire a house and the right to vote at a time when only a man owning a freehold was qualified to vote in Parliamentary elections.

Hence property advertisements such as one published in the *Surrey Comet* during July, 1866 offering nine freehold cottages, each with four rooms and a wash-house, with yard at the back, "admirably adapted for mechanics and others desirous of residing in their own freeholds, and at the same time possessing a vote in the election of MP's for Surrey."

This last inducement to buy lost its potency after the Reform Act of 1867 gave the Parliamentary vote to citizens who were householders, but not necessarily owners, in towns.

It was not only the poor of Kingston who lived in primitive conditions. To maintain competitive business hours, traders had always lived on or close to their premises. In the Market Place, and other streets of the ancient town centre, this meant that the homes of comparatively substantial citizens could be as cramped and ill-favoured as those of the lower orders.

Street directories of the period, with their detailed lists of residents, show how this pattern changed. As new housing sprang up around the town, merchants and tradesmen for the first time began leaving their homes 'over the shop' in favour of villas in Surbiton, Knights Park and Norbiton.

Still the fact remained that for many people it would always be an economic impossibility to buy their own homes. Even those who could were often dismayed to find that their houses had been built to the shoddiest specifications. For, despite the massive tide of development, there were no real controls on building standards.

It was not until 1868, after repeated lambastings from the *Surrey Comet,* that the town council conceded that it should lay down byelaws for the regulation of building. Their slowness in drawing up such bylaws, and their reluctance to enforce them once they had, was largely because so many councillors were themselves builders and/or cottage landlords. On September 29, 1866 the Medical Officer (appointed at a salary of £50 a year) boldly told the Improvement Committee that Kingston Council had "a cottage-owning element which obstructs sanitary improvements". The same point was frequently made by the *Surrey Comet.* Another factor was that tenants themselves often resisted improvements because of the consequent rise in rents. Thus the Royal Borough contained hundreds of cottages which, though new, were crowded together in squalid groups without mains water, drainage or even the common decencies. The *Surrey Comet,* inspecting newly-built properties in 1868, cited Mill Street as a typical example. Here were new houses not only without mains water or drains, but whose "outer offices were fully exposed to the view of passers-by in an adjacent footpath."

They were little better than houses in the old quarters of Kingston, described the *Surrey Comet* in 1860:

> "They are destitute of the most common necessaries for decency, one water closet being made to serve for several dwellings. Some are without a sink of any kind and the dirty water is brought out and emptied into uneven gutters and may be seen standing in fetid pools. Many possess no water supply at all, and it is much to the credit of the industrious poor that they keep their homes as clean as they do . . . many

fetch the water they use for drinking and all other purposes straight from the Thames."

Equally foul were conditions in Bridewell Alley, site of today's Fairfield Road. William Drewett, in the *Kingston and Surbiton News* of June 30, 1900 recalled it in the days of his boyhood.

"It was only wide enough for three people to walk abreast, and on fair days locomotion was difficult," he wrote. "It was a favourite pitch for the vendors of songs of the Seven Dials order, who used to exhibit their stock on long strips of canvas. These, stretched between poles, were made fast close to the Bridewell Wall."

Originally the alley ran alongside a wall of the Bridewell Prison which, after its closure in 1852, was converted into barracks for the 3rd Royal Surrey Militia. Bridewell Alley was only five foot wide and was described at a town council meeting in February 1861 as "a den of infamy with abodes of filth, shame and pollution." In 1864 the alley was replaced by Fairfield Road to provide proper access from Eden Street to the Fairfield: but evidently nothing was done to improve the houses. A townsman wrote to the *Surrey Comet* in July 1866 to express his disgust with what he saw in the Eden Street area: "However great an improvement the making of a new road may be, to my mind it would have been preferable to have swept away this nest of hovels, for they are not worthy of the name of houses, which teem with dirt and filth, and swarms with not too cleanly inhabitants. Those who have to pass the group of buildings cannot but fail to be struck at a distance with its wretchedly dirty appearance, but those who pass immediately in front must also inhale the foul exhalations."

Youngs Buildings were another shameful product of the 19th century. They were a terrace of 13 houses, approached from Eden Street through an archway and along a winding passage, seven feet wide. The houses stood in a filthy courtyard, hemmed in by the backs of buildings in Clarence Street and Eden Street, by a butcher's yard and by stabling piled high with manure. In June 1866 Kingston's Medical Officer, Mr J.G. Kent, drew attention to the fact that nearly all the privies in Youngs Buildings were full to the floor "and are frequently running over."

He made another scathing report to Kingston Board of Guardians on March 22, 1870:

"Frequently in the winter, but particularly in the summer, the place stinks, not from its own impurities alone, but from the emanations of the surrounding yards and buildings," he said, adding that seven of the houses were infected by smallpox. He found all the houses occupied by two or more families, crowded into six small rooms. The front door opened into a room 11 feet 4 inches by 10 feet 6 inches, with a stone-paved scullery at the back. There were four more rooms on the two upper floors. There was no mains water. One communal pump in the courtyard was the only supply, and those who wanted to flush their lavatories had to fetch the water from there. For this, residents paid rents ranging from 6s. 9d. to 8s. weekly, and were responsible for repairs.

Dr Henry Pitman, Medical Officer for Manchester, denounced Youngs Buildings the following week as "nothing less than a smallpox manufactory" and a danger to the crowded town centre. Unsavoury details of Youngs Buildings appeared regularly in the Press for the rest of the century.

Eventually, however, these houses managed to live down their Victorian past. They were inhabited until the 1960's, while the archway and path leading to them remained until the construction of the Eden Walk shopping precinct in the 1970's.

The horror story of Kingston's 19th century housing development can be traced detail by distasteful detail in the Medical Officers' regular reports. The council, weighed down by inertia and vested interests, did little. A reader's letter published in the *Surrey Comet* of May 6, 1871 is typical of the contempt felt for the town's leaders at this time. It makes salutary reading for anyone tempted to look back on Kingston's Victorian past through a rosy mist of illusion:

> "Occupying a first-rate position, built on the banks of the river, the focus of a large agricultural district and the centre of an aristocratic portion of Mid-Surrey, Kingston yet presents to the eye, in its public buildings, its private dwellings and its tradesmen's shops, taken as a whole, a commoness of structure, a beggarly mean-ness of design and a lowness of tone which are not rivalled in any town of a similar size in the home counties.
>
> "Let any un-biased man walk up Eden Street, and what would his opinion suggest at the unpaved roadway, the wretched hovels and the placarded walls? He would find there an amount of coarseness, intermingling with the privacy of life, which could have been expected more in Whitechapel or St Giles than in the neighbourhood of the capital of Mid-Surrey. Passing along the Fairfield, let him turn his steps down Mill Street, and turning to the left walk up Alexandra Road (note: this was re-named Denmark Road in 1880). Here it is impossible to imagine that inspectors of nuisances have ever penetrated, or that the boundaries of a parish have encircled this spot, for all that characterises the

degradation of humanity presses itself to the eye in aggravated force. A turgid rivulet on the one hand teems with putrid and obscene abominations, while on the other the 'human form divine', covered with rags, lies in hovels foul, damp and undrained, with poverty, vice and misery as bedfellows. Horrid and dismal as this neighbourhood undoubtedly is, it unfortunately does not exhaust such dreadful characteristics of our town. A little further on brings one near the cemetery, where we find the houses have been built without any apparent idea of room, comfort or convenience. And again, directly opposite the Cambridge Asylum, we are horrified to find running parallel with that noble monument of English charity, and close by it in Asylum Road, places unfit to be named as human habitations.

"Disgraceful as this spot is, it is disgraced by the road, which in winter and spring becomes an impassable swamp, and in summer the dustbin of the neighbourhood. Authority cannot plead ignorance of the state of this road, seeing that our worthy and respected Medical Officer, Mr Kent, in the discharge of his duties drew the attention of the Council to it, as well as Washington Road, which deserves a word in passing . . . it has proved itself within the last few years as a great propagator of the most virulent and fatal epidemics that the human race is subject to . . . one is compelled to confess, when contemplating the gross negligence of our local authorities in these matters, that Kingston is more indebted to a merciful providence than the efficiency of our sanitary regulations. In such neighbourhoods vice reigns triumphant and dominates, and it says little for a governing power that they have not compelled landlords of buildings to attend more to cleanliness and health."

Kingston had become slightly less malodorous with the opening of Kingston Cemetery in the fields of Bonner Hill in 1855. Prior to that, all burials had been in Kingston Churchyard and its 'overflow' in Union Street (now the Memorial Gardens). The odour of sanctity they emitted was such that the *Surrey Comet* of June 30, 1855 felt moved to explain how the innovation of cemeteries had been brought about by "disease and pestilential vapours caused by interment in the midst of populous parishes."

After the opening of the cemetery, streets of cottage homes began springing up around it. Some, especially those in and around Cambridge Road, were the worst dwellings constructed in Victorian Kingston. An appalling example was Fuller's Square, built off Cambridge Road by William Fuller, who occupied Tolworth Farm for some 50 years until his death in 1872. His 125 acres of farmland are remembered today in the name Fuller's Way.

Within months of completion, his 28 cottages in Kingston were said to be unfit for habitation, and he was ordered by the Borough Magistrates to make improvements. Evidently he never did. Many years later, in May 1896, his son, Thomas, was summoned in respect of the same properties.

It was stated in court that the only drinking water was from a communal tank in the middle of the square. The water came from the mains, but the tank had never been cleaned and was filthy. The houses themselves had bare brick floors and roofs so shoddy that in wet weather rain poured through the ceilings and filled the holes in the floors. The magistrates heard that the development was "the centre of squalor, filth and wretchedness", yet the authorities had turned a blind eye all that time. Mr Fuller was fined 14s. and ordered to put the houses in repair.

The Victorian novelist, Rhoda Broughton, uncovered some of the horrors of Kingston home life in her book *Not Wisely But Too Well,* published in 1867. She had lived at The Grove, a gracious old house on the site now occupied by Kingston Polytechnic, and Kingston, which she re-named Queenstown, is the setting of her book.

Here the heroine looks at the Back Lanes, which lay between Wood Street and the River.

> "Dreary houses, with big cracks across them; thin walls, propped up in some cases by helping beams; apologies for windows, with great hiatuses in them, filled up by filthy, bulging clouts; a clothes line, with a great many singular shaped garments, flapping in the slight cold wind, on it – having just undergone their biennial washing; a pavement of uneven stones, some round, some sharp-edged, interspersed with puddles of dirty water, hardened now by the benevolent, disinfecting ice."

A few years previously the *Surrey Comet* had given a similarly dismal picture when making yet another of its pleas for 'model cottages' for labourers.

> "Visit their homes and what do you see – the slatternly wife with disordered hair; the ragged, screaming children; the paper-patched, dirty windows and altogether an entire absence of cleanliness and comfort in the house. Is it to be wondered at that the husband is driven by such a state of things to rest his weary limbs by the comfortable fire of the

public house and there contract those habits of excess which soon become his ruin?" it asked on August 2, 1856.

Until the mid-19th century, pretty pastoral scenery was to be found within a few minutes' walk of Kingston Market Place. This changed in the 1860's.

In 1860 "building ground for villas" was being advertised in Orchard Road. This had been the site of what William Ayliffe described as "a large white house, occupied by Mrs French, and a narrow lane (French's Lane) between French's and Horn's orchards led up to the Fairfield." Orchard Road, together with the adjacent Palmer Crescent, Grange Road and Knights Park, became a favourite location for middle income professional and businessmen, able to maintain one or two servants.

In 1865, 11 acres of farm and meadow land on the south side of the Hogsmill was transformed into the Spring Grove estate. It was owned by Mr Palmer Porter, who commissioned Mr James Nightingale to draw up plans for an area bounded by the Hogsmill on the north, Green Lane on the east, Grove Lane on the south and the grounds of The Grove mansion on the west. The new roads were named Springfield, Portland and Alexandra (later re-named Denmark) and Mr Porter announced he would dispose of plots in shares "after the manner of some building societies, except that immediate possession will be given." He also announced the building of 150 houses at rents of £30 upwards.

The *Surrey Comet* hoped there would also be a supply to let from £20. It further hoped that Springfield Road might be continued across the mill stream by a bridge at the end of Knights Park, and thence along Fairfield West and into London Road.

That dream took nearly 30 years to materialise, even though it was of immense importance at a time when the Hogsmill River was a deep, fast flow, still driving the town's last water-powered flour mill and effectively dividing Surbiton and the rapidly expanding Spring Grove area from Kingston town.

William Mercer, owner of the flour mill and of much local land, realised the necessity of a bridge and offered a piece of ground and a large sum of money for it. Others, equally eager for the project, raised a further sum before putting the plan before the Corporation. To their intense disappointment, the Corporation rejected it after some of the most acrimonious exchanges ever heard in council.

"Had there been a phonograph within the council chamber when Mr Mercer's proposals were brought forward and considered, and its cylinders set to work in the same room on the day of the bridge opening ceremony, their revelations would have astonished those who sat comfortable in the thought that there had never been any trouble or unpleasantness over the bridging of the mill stream," declared the *Kingston and Surbiton News,* reporting the long-delayed opening of the bridge on February 6, 1894, and deploring the fact that Mr Mercer had been forgotten.

When Mr Mercer died in 1870, he left land and money for the bridge to his son-in-law, William Ranyard, who promised to see his wishes carried out. But eventually, when it seemed the council would never allow the bridge to be built, he gave the cash to the Richmond Road Infant School instead.

Thus Kingston ratepayers had to find the then considerable sum of £4,000 for a bridge that originally would have cost them nothing. They would have had to find still more without Mr Mercer's gift of land. The bridge, still doing sterling service today, was designed by the borough surveyor, Major Henry Macaulay, and was very advanced for its time. It is constructed on the "bowspring" system and – a great talking point in 1894 – its girders are of steel instead of iron.

Spring Grove was extended by Alfred Nuthall, who submitted his plans to the Improvement Committee in 1876. The result was a development of neat houses fronting Grove Lane and the new Alfred Road.

An auction at The Mart in London on May 26, 1868 heralded total change in that part of Kingston to the north of the new railway. Previous to that, as the octogenarian William Drewett recalled in the *Surrey Comet* of September 3, 1921, Acre Road – known as Forty Acres – had been regarded as the end of the town and there was no street lighting beyond it.

"The dwellers in Forty Acres had between them and Ham Common nothing but open fields," he wrote.

He also recalled that the thoroughfare from Richmond Road to the gates of Richmond Park was called The Kings Highway.

> "It was formerly kept in repair by the Crown and the deduction may be that at one period a right of way across private property was acquired for getting another entrance to the Royal park and hunting ground. The road was commonly known as The Kings Highway down till the time of the development of land abutting thereon from building, which led to the widening of the road, its adoption by the local authority and a new nomenclature – King's Road. That title was also given to the approach from Richmond Road to Lower Ham Road, opposite to King's Road, which had previously been called First Lane. What is now Bank Lane, further on, was known as Second Lane, and in the hedgerow which once

formed a boundary there, I have gathered white violets in the spring."

The event that spelt the doom of white violets and open fields was the sale by his trustees of the late Lord Liverpool's farm, described in Messrs Farebrother Clark's advertisement as "a pleasure farm and 103 acres."

There were two major lots. The first was "a block of land, consisting of 33 acres, part let to Dr Roots, situated within 100 yards of Kingston Station with extensive frontage to Elm Road and a proposed road of 40 feet in width passing through the centre to develop it, divided into 60 plots, 30 plots being laid near the entrance to Richmond Park with extensive frontages to Kings Road." The second was "a pleasure farm in the occupation of Mrs Looker, with farm, cottage and buildings and 44 acres of arable and pasture land abutting on the estate of the Earl of Dysart and others, with extensive frontages to the high road from Kingston to Ham and the Kings Road intersecting it."

Much of the site was acquired by the British Land Company, who by the spring of 1869 had begun covering the fields of Park Farm with the network of residential streets known today as the district of Canbury. Freehold building land "on the new road leading from Ham and Richmond Roads to Richmond Park" was advertised extensively on easy terms: "Nine tenths of the purchase money may remain on mortgage or contract at 5% to be paid in nine years by equal half-yearly instalments." By February 1884 a meeting of the Canbury Ratepayers' Association heard there were "between two and three thousand" residents living there.

A stroll around Canbury has much to interest a local historian. The many surviving datestones on the houses indicate how spasmodic was its development, and the enormous variety of their architecture shows that a wide social mix was achieved in what could be called this forerunner of the modern "overspill" area which followed the opening of Kingston's town centre station in 1863.

Volumes could be written on Canbury and its people. Here there is scope to consider only the development of Elm Road, an ancient thoroughfare existing as Hog Lane long before railways. In the Census Returns of 1851 and 1861 it has only two dwellings. In 1851 its total population is ten. Ten years later, when its name has changed to Elm Road, only five people are listed. The returns of 1871 show a great change. Elm Road now has 210 residents listed in 37 dwellings.

Previously its people had been farmworkers. By 1871 the occupations are varied. There are guards and engine drivers, porters, coachmen and a groom, bootmaker, shoemaker, sausagemaker, cordwainer, tailor and butler.

The 1881 Returns show interesting developments in the social scale and a progression from unskilled and semi-skilled workers to the highly-skilled occupations, such as printer, cabinet maker, jeweller and clerk, living alongside the chimney sweep, blacksmith and letter carrier. There is also the first appearance of small businesses in the form of a grocer, a baker, a bootmaker and mention of The Swan. There is also a far greater proportion of residents born outside the county. Some, especially the labourers, are from as far afield as Ireland and the West-country. Hog Lane, alias Elm Road, is in fact a local social and topographical history in miniature.

* * * * * * * * *

As so often in the saga of Kingston's Victorian development, much of the 'new town' of Canbury was given cavalier treatment by its developers. Elm Road was referred to as The Slough of Despond in newspapers and on August 20, 1881 the *Surrey Comet* reported that practically every resident on the British Land Co's estate had signed a petition against the wretched state of their roads and footpaths.

George Ford, born in East Road in 1885, recorded his memories of 19th century Canbury in a series of letters written before his death in 1978.

"When we lived in Gibbon Road from 1888 to 1893, the whole of the area from Richmond Road was on well or pump water," he wrote. He recalled homes where poultry ran freely in and out, and where costermongers slept with their donkeys in the front parlour at night. Few families could afford a 'kitchener' for their cooking. For simple boiling, wrote Mr Ford, they used the open fire. If baking or roasting was required, the food would be taken to Wallis the baker to be cooked in the great stone ovens which, together with the Wallis family business, still survive in Richmond Road.

The reports of Kingston Licensing Sessions are a rich source of information on population and building growth. On March 8, 1890 for example, the *Kingston and Surbiton News* account of the Sessions mentions a population of 4,350 on the Canbury estate. Reference is made to 58 houses completed in Willoughby Road, 44 in Deacon Road, 128 in Elm Road, 138 in Canbury Park Road, 28 in Shortlands Road, 24 in Osborne Road and 38 in Windsor Road. The Richmond Park Hotel has also been built in Kings Road by Fricker's Brewery on what had recently been a charming country copse known as Fir Tree Clump.

There are interesting social data in the advertisement that led to the establishment of Canbury's own parish church of St Luke. It appeared in the *Surrey Comet* of July 29, 1882 and had been placed by Archdeacon Charles Burney, together with the Vicars of All Saints and St Paul's and Mr John Galsworthy, father of the famous author.

> "At the last census, the population of the parish of St Paul's, Kingston Hill, in which the above district (Canbury) is situated, amounted to 6,280, having more than doubled since the census of 1871, and at the present rate of building it seems probable that the number may not be far short of 10,000 by the time of the next census. As the ground is being so rapidly covered with houses, it has been felt that no time should be lost in securing a site for a future church and we have much pleasure in announcing that the Rochester Diocesan Society have most liberally come forward and enabled us to purchase a suitable site in the centre of the poor population."

The group added that they hoped to purchase an iron church, with accommodation for more than 600.

> "As a large proportion of the labouring population for whose use the church which it is now sought to erect is mainly designed are engaged in work outside the parish, it is hoped that many who are not actually parishioners will be disposed to lend a hand in the present emergency."

It was a plea which aroused what had become a diminishing sense of community in Kingston. During the next decade, as perusal of the local press will show, Royalty, in the form of the Duke and Duchess of Teck, the Duchess of Albany and Princess Frederica, joined with local residents of all classes in canvassing and fund-raising for the new church. By 1883 the iron church had opened in Elm Road. By 1889 it had been replaced by the present fine building at the junction of Gibbon and Burton Roads.

From 1895 the notorious Back Lanes – described at a council meeting as "that rookery of infamy most vile, that maze of filth and debauch" – were demolished, together with the adjoining Nightingale's Brewery. A survey of the Back Lanes, published in the *Kingston and Surbiton News* on April 19, 1890, found 556 people living there, of which 201 were from the 49 artisan families in the quarter. There were also 155 single labouring men and a "migratory population" of 200, a half of which was made up of organ grinders. Only three of the Back Lanes' nine pubs were replaced in the subsequent re-development, and the brewery site was used for Kingston's first council houses.

They were built in three blocks, and each house contained a living room, kitchen and three bedrooms, together with "sanitary arrangements carried out in the most approved principles." They were built by Mr C. Skinner of Chatham for £4,794 and won much praise. Unfortunately, rents of between 8s. 6d. and 11s. 6d. put them beyond the reach of the people who had been displaced.

Warwick Deeping's novel, *Smith*, published in 1932, has Canbury Place as one of its settings under the fictitious name, Paragon Place. This area, now cleared of houses, lies between Richmond Road and the river, and in the 19th century was filled with working class cottages?

> "It was a strand in a spider's web of obscure and ugly little streets. It was built of yellow brick and every cottage had the same flat, bilious face, the same two windows front and back . . . it had been built by a man without vision for people who had not been taught to see."

But many 19th century Kingstonians could see, and they did not like what met their eyes.

The *Surrey Comet* spoke for them in its leader column of March 29, 1879:

> "It is impossible to walk through our neighbourhood without being struck by the incongruous and pretentious style of our modern architecture. Our builders either go to the extremes of utilitarian ugliness or to an excess of imitative ugliness. We have many examples of a mongrel kind of fancy architecture. Some of our best building sites are being covered with houses run up with almost electric rapidity. We have seen the bricks laid in freezing weather with steaming mortar, with the thinnest of timber stuck on end. Scamp, haste and speculation, and a genteel artistic 'style' mark these Brummagen structures that are rising up on all sides. Even many of our very best erections are violations of good taste and are showy shams, having much outside ornamentation but very little stability or good honest workmanship."

Kingston entered the 19th century as a picturesque country town, rich in historic architecture. It left it as what many of its people regarded as an undistinguished sprawl, grievously scarred by inertia, greed, vested interests and lack of vision.

A feature by Arthur Wright in the *Kingston and Surbiton News* of March 10, 1900, pulls no punches.

Regretting the "terribly mutilated and restored" All Saints' Church, Mr Wright finds only two buildings worth praise: St Raphael's Church in Portsmouth Road and Surrey County Hall in Penrhyn Road.

"But over the remainder of Kingston, in vain we seek for architecture," he writes. "Street after street of dingy bay-windowed 'suburban villas' – here a little change for the better, there for the worse, but on the whole one vast area of meaningless, monotonous bricks and mortar. In the town itself we find nothing (or practically nothing) disheartening, disgraceful, out of repair, insanitary – nothing interesting, nothing well done. 'shop room and plate glass' has evidently been the cry for the past 30 years . . . all taste, all feeling, all art is sacrifieced for the sake of show of stock. I have hunted Kingston from end to end, form hill to river, and I find no more than half-a-dozen scraps of architecture. Why is it?

"Where is there another town, village or hamlet that can boast a thousand years' popularity and has no lasting record, no monument of those who made it so? Can it be that the far famed Corporation have always had a mania for 'improvements', improvements which have resulted in narrow streets and dangerous corners, a maze of thoroughfares and awkward frontages, and which at last have brought the town to a dingy, bustling, half-awake suburb instead of our boasted 'quiet, peaceful, picturesque, ancient and loyal' borough."

Then, as now, town planners seldom found favour in their own lifetime!

The Stately Homes of Kingston

Nineteenth-century Kingston could boast some fine old mansions. Solidly built, set amid well-guarded acres of parkland, they had been conceived as lasting features of the landscape. Yet they began to disappear with startling speed once trains had steamed their way into local life.

The rush for building land was a major reason. In some instances the grounds were sold off portion by portion over the years, leaving the mansion marooned on an ever-shrinking island of garden until finally engulfed by building development. In other cases, house and grounds gave themselves up to developers in one act of surrender. Thus most Kingstonians are today living on sites with intriguingly stately connections.

Stand at the traffic-drenched junction where the London and Cambridge Roads meet. Then look at the roughly triangular area bounded by the Cambridge, Coombe and Gloucester Roads. How hard it is to imagine that this was once the noblest estate in Kingston, surrounding the elegant mansion Pope's, subsequently re-named Norbiton Place.

Local land tax books show that by 1809 the property was owned by Charles Pallmer. He is described in *Excursions in the County of Surrey,* published in 1821, as "a spirited individual and liberal benefactor to the town" who in 1819 had had the dilapidated old Kingston Bridge repaired at his own expense.

"To the same gentleman," adds the author, "Kingston is indebted for its lamps; they having been restored, at a very recent period, by his means, after an unaccountable discontinuance of so essential a convenience, for a long period of years."

Pallmer had made a fortune from sugar planting in the West Indies. Some time prior to 1821 he set about improving Norbiton Place under the guidance of Edward Lapidge, the eminent architect who later designed the handsome stone bridge that in 1828 replaced the wooden structure that had formerly served as Kingston Bridge. A splendid Ionic portico was added to the west front of the house. Then came a new wing, containing a 50-foot library. Pallmer also increased his grounds from 40 to 300 acres.

A major feature of these grounds was a lake, created by Mr Pallmer to provide employment for destitute labourers during a particularly hard winter. It was achieved by boring down 472 feet to an underground spring. The result was a splendid sheet of water which Pallmer embellished with a grotto and a handsome stone bridge.

Nothing now remains of the estate, with its three farms, its arable and sheep grazing land and its 40 acres of pleasure ground. We must rely on G.F. Prosser's *Select Illustrations of the County of Surrey,* published in 1828, for a description of the great park which Pallmer threw open to the public every weekend. It is worth quoting extensively from Prosser to show how far a wealthy man was prepared to go to create luxurious surroundings for himself in 19th century Kingston:

> "In making a circuit of the grounds, a dairy in the style of an Indian temple meets the view. This is the most tasteful of its kind in the county. The walls are lined with small slabs of Staffordshire ware, bordered by a wreath of fig leaves. The windows of ground glass are embellished by painted groups of flowers and birds; the floor is inlaid with black and white marble and a broad ledge of a species of slate stone with carved supporters in bronze continues round the apartment. A large marble Tazza from an antique Italian model stands on a sculptured stone pedestal in the centre, and a spring of water overflows from a well-executed acanthus."
>
> Mr Prosser was equally charmed by the grotto:
>
> "It comprises a bath with apartments, and is a good representation of natural rockwork. The roof pendants are extremely well managed in imitation of those natural petrifactions called stalactites, which adorn the caverns of nature. From an elevated seat, a view of the whole grotto is obtained with water issuing from the numerous interstices in its sides and ivy with other creeping plants in all the wild profusion of nature growing over it. The whole effect is very considerably heightened by the retired and sombre air which pervades the place."

He describes the "very handsome stone bridge", the fountain modelled from one in Florence and the "gold and silver lily pond, filled with water plants, which receives the stream on its descent." The house and grounds, he tells us, were ornamented with many pictures, busts and statues. The main entrance from London Road was by iron gates, hung between decorated pillars topped by sphinxes. Just inside the gates was a lodge copied from a Doric temple.

In 1836 the bottom fell out of Charles Pallmer's purse, partly because of his expenditure on Norbiton Place, but mainly because of his huge outlay on getting himself elected MP for Surrey in 1826. His estate was broken up into 27 lots and sold for the then princely sum of £19,951. A catalogue from the sale is evidence of an era when choice building land could be had for £50 an acre. It also gives interesting insights into the origins of some of Kingston's street names. Hawks Road, for instance, commemorates The Hawks, described in the catalogue as "a freehold property, forming the corner of London and Malden Road (now Cambridge Road) with extensive frontage thereon and including a brick-built homestead, a very capital barn, two granaries, excellent cattle yards and sheds and other agricultural buildings, a stackyard, a meadow of 11½ acres and a close of nearly an acre called the hop ground." All of this fetched £2,500. The pleasure grounds stretched over the area now covered by St Peter's Church (built in 1842) Norbiton Station, part of the Cambridge Estate and the densely-developed Chatham, Clevedon, Chesham and Cobham Roads and Norbiton Avenue. The great lake was approximately where Chesham and Cobham Roads are now. The "very handsome stone bridge" was at the north end of what is now Chesham Road and the grotto was at the north end of Cobham Road.

A large portion of the pleasure grounds, including the lake, grotto and dairy, was acquired for a new mansion, known as Norbiton Park, and occupied by wealthy families until 1900, when workmen demolished the house, felled the magnificent trees and filled in the lake to make way for many of the houses situated between the Coombe and Cambridge Roads. On August 15, Messrs Nightingale, Phillips and Page auctioned the demolition materials. "Good stockbricks" fetched £1 per thousand. The highest price was achieved by "ornamental railing on the bridge over the lake", which was knocked down to a town councillor for five guineas.

> "One notes with regret the disappearance of these old houses, sequestered in their richly timbered parks, to make room for rows of cheap villas; but this is an age of progress, not sentiment, and none can deny that a hundred or two of 'attractive red brick villas' will be more conducive to the prosperity of a community than one historic mansion, perhaps untenanted for a 12-month," commented the *Surrey Comet* of August 18.

And what of the Norbiton Place mansion? That survived, together with a mere five of its former 300 acres, for several more years. Its demise, however, was long and painful. The beautiful portico crumbled away. The wing was amputated. By the early 1900's it had become the White Rose Laundry. Now the site is covered by motor showrooms and other commercial buildings and nothing remains of Charles Pallmer's amazing flight of fancy.

He went into financial exile in France, dying in Boulogne in 1848. His widow returned to Kingston, settling at Palmyra Farm, Seething Wells, where she died in 1873. This little estate subsequently disappeared to make way for extensions to the Chelsea Waterworks in Portsmouth Road.

* * * * * * * * *

Today's London Road, Norbiton is heavily urbanised, with a high proportion of offices and shops; but in the 18th and much of the 19th centuries it still combined rural charm with close proximity to Kingston town, and was a fashionable residential area with elegant mansions.

Almost opposite Norbiton Place, on the north side of London Road, was Norbiton Hall. Today that means a block of flats. To 19th century Kingstonians it meant a stately home, noted for the eminence of its many owners and the splendour of its hothouse fruits.

References to the mansion date back to the 16th century. In 1829 it was jointly purchased by Mary, Countess of Liverpool, whose husband had died in Kingston the previous year after 15 years as Prime Minister, and her cousin by marriage, Robert Jenkinson. He was Lieutenant Governor of Dover Castle, but in Kingston was known as "Squire" Jenkinson because of his opulent establishment at Norbiton. William Drewett, recounting boyhood memories in the *Surrey Comet* of September 24, 1921, recalled how the "Squire" had a handsome barouche drawn by a pair of splendid greys. When he died in the mid-1850's (the Countess had died in 1846) there was a great sale at Norbiton Hall and one of the greys, Tommy, was bought by J & B Marsh, the local millers, for £70. Instead of drawing a fashinable equipage, Tommy had to pull a trader's van, and showed his displeasure and his mettle by going so fast he was a menace to the town.

As the railway age progressed, Norbiton Hall's acreage decreased as its grounds were pared away for building plots. However, they were still extensive when Norbiton Hall was acquired from John Guy in 1864 by barrister William Hardman. He quickly became a major personality in Kingston, serving as Mayor, Chairman of the Magistrates and

Recorder of the borough. In 1885 he was knighted for his long public service.

During the 1860's, Hardman wrote detailed accounts of his daily life to his old Cambridge friend, Edward Holroyd, who was practising as a barrister in Australia. In 1930 these letters were published as *The Hardman Papers*. They give vivid glimpses of what gracious country living was like in 19th century Norbiton.

Hardman was charmed to find that a stone over the entrance of his new home gave the date of its renovation and alteration as 1681. However, not having the wealth of the Jenkinson family, he had to make the beautiful grounds earn their living.

"I shall have extensive hothouses, nursery, grape and orchid houses, and am absolutely going to be rash enough to keep a head gardener and two or three under-gardeners," he wrote in October, 1864. "I look to Covent Garden as a mart for my fruit. I shall also keep cows, pigs and poultry . . . we are not going to keep horses or carriages."

He did not find his wealthy Norbiton neighbours pleasing.

> "The people in this neighbourhood call upon us freely, and I am fearfully victimised by being compelled to return said calls – a process which is in the highest degree distasteful to me," he wrote in December, 1864. "Our friend Colonel Cochran (cousin of Lord Dundonald) and his wife have amused us much by their advice as to who are the *right* people to know."

Formerly, all the mansions of Norbiton could boast the *right* people; but by the latter half of the 19th century, though the estate owners had money, they did not have the social standing of their predecessors – a fact that evidently had much to do with Hardman's appointment as a JP within five months of his arrival in Norbiton.

"I am told by a very good authority that my elevation to the Bench has flabbergasted several in the neighbourhood who are fully qualified and have been moving heaven and earth to get made magistrates for a long time," he wrote to Holroyd in March, 1865. "But the Lord Lieutenant would not consent, regarding their education and manners as scarcely those of gentlemen."

Later Hardman became chairman of Surrey Quarter Sessions, a position he held for the rest of his life, and for which he was knighted in 1885.

He soon found life in Norbiton idyllic.

> "We are daily more in love with our country residence, and all our visitors go into ecstasies about it," he wrote in 1865. "It would require the strongest inducement or the sternest

necessity to make us return to that dear, noisy, stuffy, smoky, dusty old London."

That declaration was put to the test the following year, when the Prince of Joinville offered £17,000 for the estate.

"More than twice the price I paid to Mr Guy – 8,000 guineas," recorded the incredulous Hardman. "This offer made us think deeply," but we decided to decline it after 24 hours deliberation . . . I did not think I had got the place so cheaply, or that property here would rise so rapidly in value, although I was aware that land adjoining me had been sold for £1,200 per acre during the past 12 months."

No wonder the stately homes of Kingston were shrinking! Even Sir William was so induced to compromise between love for Norbiton Hall and money. He clung to the house, but in February 1868 this announcement appeared in the *Surrey Comet:* "Norbiton Hall Estate, close to the proposed new railway station. Very desirable building land in large or small plots." In December the same year, Kingston Improvement Committee's minutes recorded that "permission was granted to build a public house on the Norbiton Hall estate."

There are many pictures and descriptions of the exteriors of Kingston's great houses but glimpses of what went on inside their walls are not so frequent. So let us savour some of William's descriptions of life at Norbiton.

"The Horticultural Exhibition came off in my garden," he writes in June 1867. "The principal tent was 180 feet in length, and it was filled with a grand collection of flowers and plants, to which my gardener contributed some of the finest specimens. There was another tent 50 feet long for the ladies' table decorations and a smaller one for fruit and vegetables. Nuthall and Sons had a tent for ices and refreshments . . . The band of the 3rd Hussars played admirably in spite of the rain. There were 42 performers. When the shilling visitors came the weather was very fine, and we had about 1,000 persons during the day . . . I have not far short of two miles of gravel walks, besides at least an acre and a half of lawn, so there was plenty of room for them . . . it is unnecessary for me to say that nothing was injured – the public respected what was intended for their enjoyment . . . Everybody was delighted, especially the shilling folks and my praises, and laudations of my grounds and liberality are in everybody's mouth. A great many people had no idea there were such beautiful grounds in Kingston."

June was obviously a busy month in Kingston's social calendar.

"We have an amazingly pleasant circle of friends here, and there is no end to the parties and visiting," continues Hardman. "Last Saturday, June 15th, we had a lawn party of croquet, three sets playing at once. At seven o'clock we all sat down to a cold dinner. No less than 43 were comfortably seated in my dining room. There was dancing afterwards till eleven o'clock. Next week our children are to have their hay-making party, and I suppose their guests will muster at least thirty."

In another letter he relates: "Yesterday we gave an afternoon croquet party. About 50 people were invited, and three parts of them came. Lunch at three o'clock, carriages at seven. Band of music and two sets of croquet."

In January 1866 Hardman writes of two dinner parties at Norbiton.

> "On the 15th we gave a large dinner party (16) to our strictly Conservative set. We had made great floral preparations in advance and astonished our visitors by our azaleas and tropical ferns and other plants. It was as good as a horticultural show. On the Saturday following we had another party also of 16 . . . I enclose you the bills of fare of both these feasts so that you may see we do the prandial business in a certain style. We had the menu printed. The dinner was entirely provided by Nuthall. The iced souffle was the best I ever tasted."

It is interesting to note that well-to-hostesses with servants at hand did not scruple to call in outside caterers like the celebrated Nuthalls of Thames Street when entertaining. It is also interesting to recall that in those days people arrested for petty offences were often not tried in court, but taken straight to the magistrates' own homes for justice. Most, like Sir William, set aside a special "justice room" to hear cases. In 1865, for instance, he writes: "My justice room here at Norbiton Hall has almost daily work, especially in the matter of drunk and disorderly and vagrants. I 'comphrehend all vagrom men' and women, and send them for various periods to the House of Correction with hard labour. They howl and groan before me in vain, they tell piteous tales to a deaf ear. It is very unpleasant work, but is very necessary, as we are just such a distance from town as to cause us to be inundated with these wretches, and the police having got a local beak in my person, constantly on the spot, are increasing their activity."

In 1875 Hardman became Editor of the *Morning Post* (now the *Daily Telegraph*) and was obliged to leave Norbiton Hall which, from the Surrey Land Owners' Returns of 1873, still had nearly 12 acres left.

In 1882 much of the garden was torn up for Birkenhead Avenue. This was the creation of Henry Harrison, who had bought Norbiton Hall as an investment while continuing to live at Maple Lodge, Surbiton (which had passed to him from his father-in-law, the railway contractor Thomas Brassey). Harrison formally opened his new road in March

1883 by taking down the barriers and travelling its length in an open carriage and pair. He named the new thoroughfare to commemorate his close family links with the town of Birkenhead. Six months later Harrison was dead, and in March 1884 his executors were advertising Norbiton Hall for sale as a house with "four servants' bedrooms, five best bedrooms, dressing and bathroom, drawing, dining, morning and billiard rooms, library, breakfast room."

The pleasure grounds had been pared to a mere two acres. The rest had been split into building lots. One, eight acres on the west side of Birkenhead Avenue, fetched £5,272. Another, two acres adjoining the house and garden, were bought by Mr E.J. Cave for £1,600. Mr Cave, who was already living at Norbiton Hall for a rent of £200 a year, also bought the house for £3,500.

A few weeks later the Bee Land Co were offering 36 plots of building land fronting Birkenhead Avenue, describing it as "old pasture land . . . studded with fine trees . . . formerly part of the Norbiton Hall estate." The land sold at £4. 5s. a square foot – described by the *Kingston and Surbiton News* as "moderate compared with other sites in the vicinity."

Thereafter Norbiton Hall, once so secluded, was hemmed in by roads and housing. In 1933, after a long decline, it made headlines when a local consortium announced plans to buy the estate and turn it into a dog racing track. Controversy raged and Kingston Council vetoed the idea. The consortium appealed to the government, but their plan was rejected. Soon afterwards the old house was demolished and replaced by 192 flats. But the name Norbiton Hall has been retained and there is a plaque on the frontage to commemorate its history.

Meanwhile Sir William, who was buried in Kingston Cemetery in 1890, is remembered in the name Hardman Road.

* * * * * * * * *

Near Norbiton Hall, on the same side of London Road, is the only one of Norbiton's stately homes to survive: Elmfield, the beautiful 18th century residence now used by Tiffin Boys' School as a library and sixth-form teaching centre.

Researches by Kingston upon Thames Archaelogical Society have proved that the site was originally a farm, owned by the neighbouring Lovekyn Chapel. In the 1750's the present house, known initially as Walnut Tree House, was built in the pale yellow stock bricks so fashionable in early Georgian times. Thereafter it became the home of various wealthy people, including the 4th Duke of Atholl. Late in the 19th century the house, re-named Elmfield, was the home of the Walbanke-

Childers family, who frequently used the beautiful grounds for garden parties and other events in aid of the new St Luke's Church at Canbury.

The estate was purchased by the Endowed Schools Committee in the 1920's for £3,800. A new Tiffin Boys' School was built in the grounds and officially opened in 1929.

* * * * * * * * *

Kingston seems to have viewed the loss of most of its gentlemen's residences with equanimity. Their beauty was, for the most part, hidden behind high walls. But there appears to have been widespread regret at the break-up of the Canbury Lodge estate.

Canbury Lodge was an attractive early 19th century house, rated in 1838 as house, offices and land of 8 acres, 2 rods. It stood near what is now the corner of Cromwell Road, with pretty parkland stretching north along Richmond Road to what is now Canbury Park Road.

Here for many years lived Dr Philip Fisher, master of Charterhouse from 1804 until his death in 1842. His three unmarried daughters, Mary, Frances and Jane, continued to live there until the arrival of the railway into central Kingston shattered their quiet retreat.

The Fisher sisters had taken part in organised protests against the railway plans. Nevertheless, Kingston Station opened in 1863 on a site almost opposite their home, and where there had formerly been a great tithe barn, surrounded by market gardens and cornfields. Plans were soon instigated to build an extension line to link Kingston with the main line at Wimbledon and provide a new station at Norbiton. The Kingston Further Extension Bill was passed in the House of Lords in 1865 and the Misses Fisher's estate was promptly bought up by the London and South Western Railway Company.

Originally, the new line was intended to traverse Richmond Road by level crossing. Then it was decided to build a high level line, spanning the road by a bridge. This stirred hopes that the Canbury Lodge park might be saved. It was not to be.

"Great changes can be looked for in this part of the town," lamented the *Surrey Comet,* on news that the estate had been sold. They were right. The railway embankment reared through the grassland where the Fishers had previously grazed cows. Cromwell Road (known first as Till's Road because a Mr E. Till was by then occupying the house) was carved through the centre of the park. The way was set for this to become one of the ugliest spots in the Royal Borough.

The house lingered on into the 20th century, latterly as the home of the Sherrard family. In 1910 the Kingston Picture Theatre (re-named

Studio 7 at the time of its demise in 1983) was built in part of the remaining garden. By 1913 the house had been renamed Canbury Croft. In 1914 it was wrecked by a gas explosion.

Today the house that inspired England's most famous landscape painter, John Constable, to reach for his sketching pad has been replaced by Kingston Bus Station, with Bentalls Depository immediately behind. (Richard Taylor, in the Kingston upon Thames Archaelogical Society's Newsletter for Summer 1983, reveals that Constable was a close friend of the Fisher family and a welcome guest at Canbury Lodge until his death in 1837.)

Probably the last description of it as anything like its former pastoral self is an advertisement published by Debenham Tewson Farmer in February, 1884:

> "A comfortable old-fashioned residence, containing on two floors 11 bedrooms, three reception rooms, conservatory, full-sized billiard room and complete domestic offices. Stabling for five horses, adjoining coach-houses and yard. The pleasure grounds are disposed in lawns studded with fine old timber trees, also kitchen and fruit gardens, greenhouses and gardener's cottage. Adjoining the above is stabling with yard, let to Mr E. Drew."

The idyll is broken by the final lines of the advertisement:

"Three shops with back premises in London Street now in hand and a timber yard, adjoining the cartway entrance to Canbury Lodge. The whole covers an area of about four acres and is ripe for immediate development as a building estate at small cost, being almost surrounded by roads."

William Drewett, in memories published in the *Surrey Comet* gives glimpses of Canbury Lodge and its occupants as he recalled them in the 1850's.

"It was in olden times a compact and valuable estate, with a frontage to Richmond Road extending to Hog Lane (now Canbury Park Road) . . . it was owned and occupied by three sisters, Fisher by name, who took a keen interest in every movement for the general good, and especially in the schools near them. It was their custom to spend a month at Cromer each summer and make the journey, about 150 miles, in their own carriage, going by post stages. That was regarded as a great undertaking . . . a special farewell visit was paid to the girls' school in Richmond Road on the eve of starting, and there was always an assemblage of neighbours to see the travellers pass out of the carriage gateway."

* * * * * * * * *

Pause at the pedestrian crossing where Clarence Street meets London Road, and picture the scene that existed here a hundred years ago – a peaceful scene of velvet lawns, prize blooms and, incredibly, a farm yard stacked high with local corn where C & A stands now.

On the spot occupied by the Empire Theatre, now converted into the Reject Shop, stood Canbury House. It was a fine old mansion that was the home of the Roots family from 1784 to the early 20th century.

The Roots were one of the most distinguished families in the annals of Kingston, making their mark in the fields of medicine, the law and history (a good account of their origins and achievements is given in the *Surrey Comet's* obituary of Dr Sudlow Roots, in the issue of July 22, 1876). Their house was built in the mid-17th century and was said to boast the fine Spanish chestnut timbering that was a feature of several houses in Kingston. Its grounds originally stretched from the corner of Wood Street, opposite Kingston Station, to a spot approximately where the Mothercare shop is now.

This stretch is so heavily urbanised it is difficult to picture it in former days. Once again we must rely on William Drewett.

> "It was one of the fine old gardens of which several were to be found in Kingston," he wrote. "Here were cultivated the fig, the medlar, quince and mulberry, with all other kinds of fruit. Well-trained trees abounded, and its chrysanthemums and fruit were so excellent that they won prizes in shows all over London."

Opposite the mansion, on what is now the C & A site, was a farm yard where the Roots housed the corn they grew in such abundance in the fields they rented at Cowleaze Farm. These fields fronted Richmond Road and stretched from Acre Road (known as Forty Acres) to Kings Road (known as The Kings Highway). William Drewett describes how, after harvest, the corn was taken to the yard and built up in round sheaves on a platform supported by stone "staddles", some of which remained years after the yard had been sold for re-development in 1877, following the death of Sudlow Roots.

Canbury House and its gardens remained some 40 years after its farm and fields had disappeared; but its death knell sounded in 1906 when Dr William Roots decided to sell. Agents were quick to see its potential.

> "Frontage of 345 feet. Available for the erection of first-class shops, a theatre, music hall or other public building," proclaimed the advertisement for the auction on November 6.

> It describes Canbury House as a "fine old-fashioned family residence, with 12 bed and dressing rooms, three large reception rooms, servants' hall and stabling for five horses." The grounds included extensive outbuildings, greenhouses and forcing pits and were particularly recommended to "syndicates, capitalists and private speculators."

The garden enjoyed a last burst of glory. Shortly before the sale, its fruit caused a sensation by winning seven prizes at the Kingston show.

Then the breakers moved in and the house was replaced by the Empire Theatre. Every major British variety star was to perform in this theatre between its opening in 1910 and its closure in 1955.

* * * * * * * * *

Richmond Road was formerly known as Canbury Lane. Like London Road, it combined country peace and beauty with proximity to Kingston town centre, and became a favoured place for the building of opulent rural retreats.

Today a prominent landmark in Richmond Road is University Motors, on the corner of Albany Park Road. On this spot once stood the entrance lodge and gates to one of the famous homes of Surrey, known variously as Point Pleasant, Mount Pleasant, Bank Farm and Bank Grove. It was created in 1797 by the great English architect, John Nash, for Major General Henry St John, son of the 2nd Viscount St John and MP for Wootton Bassett. This glorious retreat had grounds landscaped by the celebrated Humphrey Repton and a river frontage of more than a quarter-of-a-mile.

By 1821 Bank Grove had become the home of Sir John Delves Broughton, 7th baronet, and great uncle of the celebrated Victorian novelist, Rhoda Broughton. He seems to have been a more flamboyant personality than the General.

> "He was one of Kingston's celebrities," recalls George Ayliffe in his reminiscences. "He was a stout gentleman, dressed in the fashion of coaching days, and his splendid coach and four, with liveried grooms, was one of the sights of the town."

Sir John was proud of his skill with horses, and on Sundays took the whip himself to race his family to Kingston Parish Church in a brake. However, according to Frederick Merryweather's *Half a Century of Kingston History,* Sir John found time to halt a few yards short of the church to help prisoners held in the debtors' jail. This stood in Clarence Street, on a site long since covered by Bentalls. The Corporation owned the prison, but provided no food for the inmates. They were obliged to sit at the low, latticed windows, begging passers-by to "remember the poor debtors."

The poor debtors became poorer still when Sir John quarrelled with the churchwardens and never worshipped in Kingston again. After that, recalled George Ayliffe, he drove instead to Hampton Wick church in a smart turn-out with a pair of postillions and silver harness.

Sir John died in 1847, and the following year Bank Grove was bought by William Byam Martin, known throughout Kingston as "Squire Martin" because of the opulence of his life style. William Drewett has recorded how the "Squire" drove out from his estate each day in a magnificent equipage drawn by four greys, and attended by postillions in blue and silver liveries.

Squire Martin took great pride in the grounds of Bank Grove, filling the hothouses with a collection of exotics that became internationally known for their rarity and loveliness. William Keane's *Beauties of Surrey,* published in 1849, gives a detailed description of the grounds, which included elaborate walks, rose gardens, peach house, two vineries and an "elegant temple" overlooking the Thames.

After Squire Martin's death in 1870, the estate was sold for £7,325 to Charles Freake, a close associate of the Royal family. Freake, born in 1814 and created a baronet in 1882, achieved his position and wealth through what his obituary in the *Surrey Comet* of October 11, 1884 described as "his indomitable perseverance."

Social events at Bank Grove, magnificent though they were, were seldom reported in the Press. The Freakes feared that might be vulgar. However, a garden fête organised by Mrs Freake in July 1871 did find its way into the *Surrey Comet;* for the guest of honour was Queen Victoria's newly-married daughter, Princess Louise making her first public appearance with her bridegroom, the Marquis of Lorne, after their honeymoon.

Though lavishly appointed, Bank Grove was comparatively small for a house of its class. It had only 14 bedrooms, for example, and one principal reception room. Its real claim to fame was its eventual 16 acres of garden, internationally celebrated for its landscaping and rare plants.

"No written description, however graphic, can adequately convey a full idea of the magnificence of these grounds," wrote a visitor in 1881. The camellias were especially fine. Other features were the American garden, ablaze with rhododendrons, the ornamental temple, used as a summer house, and, on a more practical level, the private waterworks constructed on the far side of the estate.

After the death of Sir Charles in 1884, 14 acres of the estate were split into lots and sold during the ensuing years as building plots.

"Natural grounds, owing their beauty to time and to the labour of generations of gardeners," said the advertisement for an auction on June 20, 1886.

The house itself, with its remaining two acres, survived until 1907 as a high-class members establishment, opened in 1890 as the Albany Club. It was mysteriously destroyed by fire. Today Grosvenor Gardens, Albany Park Road and flats and houses in Lower Ham Road and Richmond Road have replaced Bank Grove and its landscaping. However much of its original boundary wall survives in Lower Ham Road, as do some of the magnificent cedars which shaded the Royal guests at Lady Freake's garden parties.

* * * * * * * * *

Adjoining the estate of Bank Grove was that of Chestnut Grove. It extended from Bank Lane to Lower Kings Road (formerly known as Second Lane and First Lane respectively) and lay between Richmond Road and the river. The house was named after the magnificent avenue of chestnut trees leading up to the main entrance; but it was also known locally as Flint Lodge because of the quaint little building by the entrance gates in Richmond Road. It was circular in shape, faced with flints, and was occupied by a married couple – he a gardener on the estate and she the gatekeeper.

"It was an odd place for a human abode, being only of one floor, with the sleeping apartments underground, access to which used to be from the outside," recalled William Drewett, writing in the *Kingston and Surbiton News* of April 17, 1897.

For most of the 19th century, Chestnut Grove was owned by the Kent family. They ceased to live there in the 1830's and it was occupied by a series of tenants. One was Mr Stovin, a director and traffic manager of the London and South Western Railway, who made what was described as "a sudden and unannounced flight to America" in 1852. Both his home and his job were then taken over by Archibald Scott, who became one of the most able and influential figures in the history of the railway company. He was succeeded at Chestnut Grove by the Dowie family, whose daughter married the Revd Henry P. Measor, Vicar of Kingston. After that, the house was taken by Col Cochrane, founder of the 12th Surrey Rifle Volunteers in Kingston.

By 1895 the estate had been bought by the British Land Society for house building. In May of that year the Improvement Committee of Kingston Council made efforts to preserve the wonderful chestnut avenue "for the delight of coming generations". The terms were too high. The avenue was destroyed and only the name Chestnut Road reminds us that it ever existed.

* * * * * * * * *

Woodbines Avenue, a pleasant residential thoroughfare between the Penrhyn and Portsmouth Roads, takes its name from Woodbines, an estate bounded by the present Portsmouth, Surbiton and Penrhyn Roads and the Bittoms.

The Queen Anne mansion, formerly known as Clock House, stood close to the Portsmouth Road, overlooking the river, and some of its foundations are said to survive in the garden of a house on the corner of Woodbines Avenue and Portsmouth Road.

From 1793 the mansion was occupied by Edward Fuhr, whose sister had married the Town Clerk of Kingston, Charles Jemmett. After Mr Fuhr's death, his executors sold the house in 1803; but in 1827 it was bought back into the family by Charles Edward Jemmett, and remained in Jemmett ownership until sold to Surrey County Council for the building of Surrey County Hall in 1892.

The Jemmetts were virtually hereditary Town Clerks of Kingston, three succeeding generations holding the office for about a century from 1747. They did not live in Woodbines, but leased it from 1841 to William Christy, a famous hatter whose label is still a feature of smart men's shops today. In 1873 Woodbines was leased to Sidney Nash Castle, a timber merchant, who went bankrupt after 1880.

The mansion survived until the early 1900's. Its grounds were gradually sold off in the years before and after. Now the estate is covered by Surrey County Hall and the Christian Science Church in Penrhyn Road, by Woodbines Avenue and Milner Road and by several flats and houses in Portsmouth Road.

* * * * * * * * *

Near Woodbines, fronting the east side of Penrhyn Road, was The Grove, a comfortable old house whose 23 acres included farm, orchard, paddock, lawns and pleasure gardens.

It was occupied for many years by Mary Fassett. Her father was owner of Surbiton Hall, where she was born in 1800.

Penrhyn Road was so named in the 1890's, in honour of the chairman of Surrey County Council, Mr E.H. Leycester Penrhyn. It is now a major thoroughfare. In Miss Fassett's time it was Grove Road, a pretty rural place bordered by fields and fine trees.

Miss Fassett's death in 1861 brought swift changes. She was buried on April 8. Within five days, Nightingale Page and Phillips were advertising the auction of The Grove estate.

"As a building speculation the situation, extent and other numerous advantages make it by far the most promising that has ever occurred, or can occur, in this locality," declared the advertisement.

Most of the advertised 23 acres were consumed by Grove Crescent, Fassett Road and several substantial villas. However, Miss Fassett's house, and a portion of its garden, remained for another 90 years or so.

In 1866 The Grove was occupied by Capt William Dawes Malton, who invited William Hardman there in 1866. Hardman mentions the visit in *The Hardman Papers,* describing The Grove as "a very nice, old-fashioned house, to which Malton has added a room in order to accommodate a very fine organ, sacred music being his great hobby."

Rhoda Broughton gives us a more detailed description in her novel, *Not Wisely but Too Well,* published in 1867.

> ". . . a grand, staring, square white house, with plenty of stucco and a portico and a good many green blinds," she writes. "Let us look into the drawing room . . . two drawing rooms, indeed, opening one into another with imposing folding doors, and an aviary at the end full of shrill-voiced canaries that sang fit to stun – fit to deafen – one . . . it looked as if a large family had been living and sitting and romping in this room for a good many years. However, there was a great warm fire and a lot of armchairs. It felt very hot and cosy. There was a pleasant smell of sandalwood workboxes and attar of roses and that subtle, vague odour that women delight in."

Evidently The Grove was a real home, not just a rich man's showplace.

* * * * * * * * *

Bentalls garage and multi-storey car park in Wood Street and the Steadfast headquarters on Thames-side stand on much of the site once occupied by the house and grounds of Down Hall. In the 15th century this estate belonged to Robert Skerne whose wife, Alice, was reputedly the natural daughter of Edward III and his mistress, Alice Perrers. Two fine brasses of the Skernes survive in All Saints' Church, Kingston.

For many years, Down Hall was the home of the Nuthall family, famous for their catering and restaurant business in Kingston and, in the person of Betty Nuthall, a noted tennis player.

Inroads into the estate were made early in the 1860's, when the London and South Western Railway brought their line over the Thames from Hampton Wick, through Down Hall meadows and Fitts Market Gardens to the present site of Kingston Station. Another slice of Down Hall went in the 1880's for the building of sewage works. In 1934 the remainder of the estate was auctioned by Nightingale Page and Bennett and bought by Bentalls for £3,950.

> "People crowded into the Kingston Hotel to learn its fate, and there was an audible sigh when a few of the older residents heard the last sharp tap of the fateful hammer and realised all that it meant for the spacious lawns, the avenue of chestnut trees, not in perfect blossom, and the quaintly planned old house which had ten bedrooms," reported the *Surrey Comet* of May 17.

On the Streets

Many pictures of Victorian street scenes in Kingston have survived to evoke nostalgia for past charms. However, the people who walked those streets a century ago had to contend with the unpleasant features that lay beneath that surface appeal.

Like most urban areas of the period, post-railway Kingston stank and so did the majority of its inhabitants. This was partly due to industry. The scents from several breweries mingled with those from the gin distillery, the candle factory and the mighty smell from the tannery in Bishop's Hall.

Worse than all of these, however, was the all-pervading stench of sewage. Those who endured it have left vivid descriptions. A letter in the *Surrey Comet* of August 18, 1855 complains of "a black, stinking and hideous deformity that has rolled down Coombe Lane untouched and unisolated for 18 years." This filthy tide was an open sewer "for all the unimaginable, abominable stuff that a large workhouse and crowded infirmary can pass forth." Another open sewer, ten feet deep ran between what is now the Eden Walk shopping complex and Eden Street. In fact, foul open ditches and overflowing cesspools were all over the borough.

Presenting his annual report in 1866, Kingston's Medical Officer, Mr Kent, said that in many houses in the town centre there was an abominable stench from overflowing sewage. In Acre Road and Cowleaze "the stench from the Latchmere Ditch is beyond words to describe." This ditch was known to local residents as "the curse of Cowleaze." It was said to be 12 foot wide and 12 foot deep "and could be scented from the tower of All Saints' Church". The problem remained until the ditch was covered in during the development of Canbury into a large residential estate.

There were noxious conditions in some of the genteel roads off Kingston Hill, where Mr Kent reported that sewage from the privies made living in some houses "all but unbearable." New Malden was even worse. Mr Kent found that the sewage for the entire area was carried along the main street in an open ditch, "the smell from which is almost intolerable," before emptying into a small stream at the foot of Coombe Hill.

Mr Kent condemned local builders, who ignored the necessity for pure air by fitting the "smallest apartment" in houses with windows that would not open.

"The consequence of this is apparent – very imperfect ventilation; and many a fever case is a most expensive one to the parish for weeks, and perhaps ultimately dies, from this faulty construction."

An inescapable feature of the Market Place was the "noxious effluvia" from the urinal in the Market Hall.

"It reeks in unmitigated nastiness," declared the *Surrey Comet* of November 30, 1867, describing it as "an eastern caravanserai, right where meat and food are for sale."

It was a scent familiar to the highly respectable owner/occupiers of Orchard Road, Grange Road and Knights Park. Fund-raising entertainments at the Drill Hall, built in Orchard Road for the 12th Surrey Rifle Volunteers in 1862, attracted audiences of 1,500 a night. But the premises had no public conveniences. The result, as reported in the *Surrey Comet* of June 12, 1880, was that the adjacent roads became "a perfect swamp."

Then there was the smell from the mortuary in Union Street. In 1887 more than 400 residents, including all the doctors in the parish, signed a petition stating that "the present shed which is called a mortuary is unfit."

At a parish vestry meeting, reported in the *Kingston and Surbiton News* of April 16, 1887, it was stated that part of the building served as a fuel store for the parish church. When warm water was needed, the only course was to "run about the streets to beg a bucketful." Conditions were such that people often refused to have their dead put there. The Coroner, Mr Braxton Hicks, told of an instance where seven people had lived and slept in one room with a corpse because the mortuary was so bad. The Vestry decided that the mortuary was "an abomination not fit for a body to be put in" and voted to adapt and improve the building, which had originally been the town's watch-house, built in 1825. (In the 1950's it was given an upper floor, a mock Tudor exterior and converted into the attractive little shop that adjoins the Memorial Gardens today).

No doubt this, and countless other sanitary evils, was a prime factor in the rise in Kingston's death rate.

In 1866 the Corporation's Medical Officer pro tem, Dr Price Jones, said that two years previously the local mortality rate had been 24 in every thousand. Now it had risen to 33 and a third, compared with the London rate of 13.

He reported cholera in The Bittoms, the Wanderings and the Workhouse and "a prevalence of diarrhoea almost everywhere." There was little improvement in this last condition as the century advanced. Twenty-five years later the *Kingston and Surbiton News* of May 9, 1891, was reporting that death from diarrhoea in Kingston during the previous year had risen to .94 compared with .56 for England and Wales.

By 1881 water closets had substantially displaced the obnoxious open privies. However, this development was not as beneficial as it should have been. In his report on the health of Kingston in 1881, the Medical officer, Mr Shirtliff, condemned "the odious and extremely frequent practise of using the same water cistern for domestic purposes and flushing the lavatory. In every case a separate flushing box should be provided for very obvious reasons."

He also called for the gaps between the pebbles in the Market Place to be filled in.

"At present they are so many reservoirs of foul-smelling filth," he declared.

From the 1860's, sewage disposal was a grave problem. The cesspool system had served when the population was of little more than village proportions. It was dangerously inadequate when numbers increased so dramatically. The Act for the Improvement of Towns obliged corporations to supersede cesspits by properly constructed drainage systems, the proceeds from which had either to flow into a convenient river or be collectd on sewage farms.

In 1862 Kingston organised a competition for the best drainage system, eventually selecting the entry from a Mr Despard for draining the borough into one main intercepting sewer that would empty itself north of Kingston railway bridge into the Thames. The Thames Conservators thereupon brought an action to prevent Kingston from disgorging its sewage into the river on the grounds that it would be "an injurious nuisance." After an immensely long hearing, resulting in no fewer than 2,500 printed pages and much national publicity, Vice-Chancellor Wood gave judgement in favour of Kingston in June 1865.

The Corporation duly pressed on with the project, and work was almost complete when, in 1867, came catastrophic news: London's four million inhabitants were to take all their water from the Thames and in future no sewage was to be discharged into the 140 miles of river above the capital from Lechlade to Putney . . . It was a blow to Kingston and all the other places who had only recently been obliged by law to spend huge sums diverting their sewage into the Thames. Their rage was increased by the fact that London itself could still continue to disgorge sewage into the river, but any town up river who did so would be fined £100 a day.

It was the start of a 25-year nightmare. Sewage disposal became the topic of the day, occupying newspaper columns year after year and forming the chief topic of conversation at social gatherings.

As Frederick Merryweather put it in his *Half a Century of Kingston History,* "At every luncheon or public dinner . . . the delectable sewage question came in with the dessert."

Eventually Kingston and Surbiton came to an agreement with the Native Guano Co., which opened sewage works in Down Hall Meadows in 1888. Mayors from many towns in Britain, together with journalists from more than 60 newspapers, gathered for an open day in 1889 to see machines – made by Willans and Robinson of Thames Ditton – working with a special chemical to separate sewage into a clear liquid, pure enough to go into the Thames, and a firm sludge that was dried, ground and sold as fertiliser. Kingston Corporation said it was "flushed with victory" at the thought that their problems had been solved by the Native Guano Co. for a mere 1½d. in the pound rate for the building of the works and 3d. in the pound for the sewage treatment. The Native Guano Co. replied that Kingston had been "letting a gold mine go into the river."

The new scheme was a blessing, too, to Hampton Wick, which was soon shooting its sewage to the works over the nearby railway bridge by means of a Shane's ejector. And there was something piquantly appealing in the thought that the sewage from 35,000 Kingstonians should have become elevated to the status of a British export, prized by international growers. The townspeople were told through the Press of their part in producing bumper harvests in Singapore and increasing the growth of sugar in Barbados – just two of the places where hundreds of tons of Native Guano were sent each year.

The Native Guano Co. even entertained guests to luncheon on the edge of the main ventilation shaft to demonstrate there was no smell.

This fragrant state of affairs did not last. As the population grew, so did the processing problems. Finally the stench from the sludge drying operation so permeated the town that the Corporation had to terminate the company's lease in 1909. It moved to Southall and paid Kingston two shillings a ton to send its sludge to them by barge for conversion into the rich brown granules that were such a boon to local gardeners.

But during the quarter-century that the sewage debate continued, Kingston had to manage its drainage as best it could.

"Many districts are fast growing with no provision for sewage but cesspools," reported Kingston Council in a desperate appeal to the Government in 1880. "Cesspools are dug by the side of their wells in a porous soil. As one cesspool is filled, another is dug, and thus a perfect honeycomb of cesspools presents a daily increasing and pregnant comment on omnia est santos."

Or, as the *Surrey Comet* cheefully put it: "The glass of water which looks so clear and sparkling to the eye may, when placed under the microscope, be found infected with millions of repulsive organisms of the most ugly and monstrous types . . . some of their extraordinary functions seem to be specially devoted to the diffusion of cholera, typhoid fever and the various types of epidemic diseases."

Even 50 years after the construction of two major waterworks in Portsmouth Road, thousands of Kingston households were still reliant on pumps and wells and there was no continuous supply to those lucky enough to have taps. In May 1891 Lambeth Waterworks Co. were announcing that their water service in the upper part of the borough would be from 5 a.m. to 9 a.m. in winter and 6 p.m. to 8 p.m. in summer. In the lower parts of Kingston, water was on tap between 9 a.m. and 4.30 p.m.

The dubious personal hygiene of Kingstonians was another factor that put the Royal Borough into bad odour. Throughout the century the majority of households had no bath, which prompted three local men – Messrs Frederick Gould, William Walter and Samuel Baker – to convert the town's former debtor's prison into a public bath house. An advertisement in the *Surrey Comet* during October 1855 describes "warm baths for the poor at 4d. each", together with "Every description of baths, hot and cold, plunge, shower and medicated."

Portable baths could be sent to all parts of the town and a professional shampooer was also provided. To no avail. Two leaseholders were ruined before the premises (after which Bath Passage is named) closed in 1862 and were converted into public lavatories.

"We could not get the people to come and have a bath, even if we gave them tickets for nothing," mourned Frederick Gould in a reminiscent interview published in the *Surrey Comet* on July 28, 1900.

Thus it was for reasons of hygiene, rather than natation, that a few of the more enlightened townsmen began campaigning for the building of swimming baths. A prime mover was Councillor Van der Pant, a respected dentist. In a council meeting reported by the *Surrey Comet* of January 3, 1880 he pointed out that the poor were supplied with coal, soup and blankets "but no means of being clean." And it was not only the poor who never bathed.

"Every class is suffering from this omission, especially ladies, who aren't allowed to swim except under cover," said Councillor Van der Pant.

After much controversy, Kingston's first swimming bath opened in July 1882. It was an ingenious design by John Dixon, the engineer whose most famous achievement was bringing Cleopatra's Needle to London. He lived in a handsome house overlooking the river in Portsmouth Road (the building is now divided into Anglesea Lodge and The Limes) and designed a giant river pontoon with a bath in the shape of a grating suspended in the middle. This grating could be raised or lowered to provide a variety of depths. The structure was built by James Lobb of Kingston for £1,000 and moored in the river near Clattern Bridge. It was formally opened on July 31, 1882. Admission was 2d. or 4d., according to the time of day, and 1d. at night. There was no mixed bathing, the bath being "set aside for females" three days a week from 10 a.m. to 4 p.m.

The superintendent was Mr David Pamplin. His article on bathing and hygiene, in the *Kingston and Surbiton News* of May 24, 1884, described how the townspeople regarded hot weather as an excuse for a general spring-cleaning of the body.

"Some still bear the almost indelible marks of their long neglect, but in the course of a few weeks the cleaning will have ceased, offering the bather time to attend more closely to the exercise of swimming." said Mr Pamplin.

He reported that 200 penny bathers a night had used the bath during its first season.

Most, he reported, got straight back into their clothes without drying their bodies. Others used "bits of dirty lining, pieces of rag, old socks and pocket handkerchiefs of various hues and degrees of dirt," as towels.

"All this and much worse I have seen among those in whom habits of cleanliness and decency should have been inculcated," he said. "I therefore strenuously advise the loan of a towel and bathing drawers for the entrance charge of one penny. In the present generation some enthusiasm has set in (and not too early) among the upper classes in favour of cleanliness, or rather perhaps I should say the use of the bath, and one is pleased to see it descending, though its progress is not as rapid as might be wished."

In October 1897 Kingston Corporation replaced its floating bath with a land-locked one in Wood Street.

Rabid dogs were a dangerous feature of Kingston streets. Bites from infected animals had led to so many cases of the usually fatal disease, hydrophobia, that in 1885 the Metropolitan Police ordered that dog owners should muzzle their animals and that all strays should be rounded up. Evidently Kingston largely ignored the instruction. On March 20, 1886 the *Kingston and Surbiton News* noted the "very large numbers of stray dogs" and the fact that owners still allowed their animals to follow them about without a muzzle.

"It is a positive nuisance created and perpetrated by people taking about what they call their 'pet' dogs. But what about the unhappy victims of the bite of these 'pet' creatures?"

The following month the paper announced that 373 cases of hydrophobia caused by dogs had been reported in the London area.

"We have in Kingston and Surbiton perhaps the greatest number of houseless dogs and vagabonds to be met with in the vicinity of London," complained the leader column of April 3.

During the next few weeks, 605 stray dogs were rounded up in the town.

It was a long-standing problem. In 1865 Kingston Corporation circulated leaflets warning that the police had been empowered to round up and destroy any dogs roaming without muzzles. No such precautions were taken in Surbiton, where many people received bites from infected animals. The *Surrey Comet* of June 3 recommended trying to save life by "fumigating the victim in a hot vapour bath" and afterwards "to keep up a copious perspiration in bed." On April 6, 1889 the *Surrey Comet* reported that PC Copping "who was severely bitten last week while removing a collie dog from the shop of Messrs G. and C. Nuthall in Thames Street, has proceeded to Paris by order of the police authorities, where he will be treated by M. Pasteur."

In Kingston, at any rate, it seems to be a myth that Victorian children were seen but not heard. From the 1850's the *Surrey Comet* complained repeatedly about youngsters intimidating and attacking people in the streets. On October 24, 1857, for example, it was carrying news of youngsters beating up pedestrians on Surbiton Hill. This problem increased. The leader column of January 22, 1881 was devoted to the shortcomings of the young:

"Seeing how severely we are mulcted to provide elementary education for the children of the poor and working classes, it is to say the least of it disappointing not to be able to discover any improvement in their manners," it declared, adding that such children learnt all the vices of life and went from childhood straight into premature manhood to become "an intolerable nuisance" to society.

The *Surrey Comet* described how they swore, smoked, intimidated pedestrians, "destroyed everything and anything of beauty" and scrawled "disgustingly obscene specimens of their calligraphy on walls."

"Even when their tastes are humoured, they mark their appreciation in such an uproarious and unruly manner that fainthearted managers of popular entertainments give up the experiment in disgust. With our craze for education, we certainly ought not to neglect, in the elementary schools, instructions in those proprieties which are always attended to in those of high degree."

On July 2 of the same year the leader column regretted the indifference of people, especially the middle classes, to the religious teaching of the young.

In fact, religion added to the babel on the streets, especially after the formation of Kingston United Gospel Army in 1882. The *Surrey Comet* of October 28, 1882 explained how it had been launched at the home of Mr J. Cooper in Fairfield Road for the express purpose of filling the all-too-many empty places of worship in the town.

It was open to recruits from all denominations and the object was "the conversion of souls by means similar to the Salvation Army." The 'troops' had to battle bravely for their cause. Their first public appearance was in October, when they marched through the main streets bearing banners and bells and stopping at all pubs and prominent corners to preach. In that, and most of their subsequent expeditions, they were jeered at, pelted with pebbles and knocked to the ground – often by soldiers of the military variety.

The Salvation Army earned even more approbrium, especially after the prohibition of street cries on Sundays came into force in October 1888.

"It is much to be desired that the brawling of the Salvation Army be stopped also," declared the *Kingston and Surbiton News* of October 13, railing bitterly against the Salvationists' "banging of tambourines and discordant howling."

On December 1, the paper remarked that the prohibition of street cries on Sundays had indeed been a boon to residents.

"But since costermongers, fish hawkers and milk and news vendors have been silenced, the Salvation Army seems determined to assert its right to disturb the quietitude of Sunday. As if the raving which passes with them for exhortation, and the discordant howling which they are pleased to call singing were not enough, there is now added a cornocopean. The din is simply hideous and ought not to be tolerated."

Even the dulcet tones of All Saints' bells concealed hostile attitudes far removed from modern notions of Victorian piety.

On February 23, 1856 the *Surrey Comet* reported a meeting,

organised by the Mayor at the request of the artisans of Kingston, to petition against the opening of places of public amusement on Sunday, so it could be a day of rest. To a packed audience, Mr T. Emms said the desecration of the Sabbath was mainly due to the example set by the higher classes, mentioning as an instance the ringing of the church bells on Sunday mornings.

The ringers, he said, were called "to labour hard and very hard." While they were ringing "they swore and sweated and rang and swore."

A serious hazard on the streets of Kingston was the large number of soldiers who were continually billetted in the town. The obligation to lodge and feed troops had been a thorn in Kingston's side in previous centuries, notably during the 17th century Civil Wars. During the 19th century it became an almost intolerable nuisance, making the streets unsafe at times and imposing great hardships on local inn-keepers.

One reason for these frequent military invasions was that Kingston was on the line of march from Woolwich to Aldershot. Another was that, in 1854, the former County Gaol for Surrey had been converted into the headquarters of the 3rd Royal Surrey Militia, predecessors of today's Territorial Army Volunteer Reserve (the Gaol, on the east side of Eden Street, had closed in 1852 and the prisoners were transferred to Lambeth). Thus the town had to play host to regular soldiers and their horses as they moved to and from the garrison at Aldershot and the arsenal at Woolwich, and to the hundreds of militiamen who converged on Kingston for annual training sessions.

The impact of the Militia on Kingston was described by the *Surrey Comet* of May 31, 1862. Commenting on the "extra row and tumult they occasion as they throng the streets of an evening", the paper said the men were of a very low class, consisting mainly of costermongers and labourers. They were lodged in pubs at an average of 14 to 16 at each house.

"No men could be decent when huddled together in this way," said Sir George Lambert at a public meeting to discuss the possibility of building barracks in Kingston. There were two such meetings in 1862, reported in the *Surrey Comet* on August 2 and September 6. They were the result of two petitions sent to the Secretary of State for War – one from the Mayor and Corporation and the other by magistrates and other influential residents of Kingston and Surbiton – respecting the 3rd Royal Surrey Militia's conduct during training.

Sir George reported that in recent years the militiamen had been mere boys from the lowest part of Lambeth. Their conduct was so destructive that it was unsafe to let children go out. He cited the Oak

Tavern in Maple Road, which had 14 men forced on them, though they had room only for 10. Here the unwanted guests pulled the bedding to bits and stole food and cutlery. The Plough at Surbiton had to take 16 men who got drunk, fought and brought in prostitutes overnight. The Royal Oak in Wood Street had to lodge no fewer than 23.

A survey revealed there were 79 public houses in the town with a total of 305 beds to quarter nearly 900 men. The sum of 2½d. a day was all the government would allow in payment.

The meeting further complained that the Militia was always followed into Kingston by thieves and prostitutes. The men were of the lowest class and foulest language, who kept respectable people away from the town. Accompanying them were between 300 and 400 camp followers who were "the scum of Lambeth."

Kingston eventually achieved a barracks in 1875. It was built on the northern edge of the town, adjoining the old homestead of Park Farm.

The old Militia buildings were demolished, and replaced by shops and houses fronting Ashdown Road, Eden Street and the south side of Fairfield Road. Meanwhile the new barracks became the head-quarters of the 31st Regimental District, and housed the 1st and 2nd battalions of the new East Surrey Regiment.

The barracks, of which only the gatehouse now remains in Kings Road, eased the problem of militiamen. But Kingston was still left with the burden of troops in transit.

A meeting of Kingston Licensed Victuallers Protection Society, recounted in the *Surrey Comet* of February 8, 1872 there had been 1,942 soldiers and 2,126 horses whom local publicans had been compelled by the terms of the Mutiny Act to accommodate. For men on the march, licensed victuallers were paid 12½d. per man and 1s. 9d. per horse. For this they had to provide a hot meal containing 1¼lbs meat, 2 pints small beer, 1lb vegetables and salt and pepper, plus a candle and a bed. For a soldier quartered in the town for a longer period, instead of merely passing through, landlords received 4d. per man for bed, light and use of cooking utensils. This, the meeting was told, resulted in a loss to the landlord of at least 8½d. per day per soldier and 3d. per day per horse.

Woe betide any publican who did not fulfil his unwanted duties to the letter. The *Surrey Comet* reported a typical instance on August 9, 1857 when the landlord of the Griffin, Mr John Williams, was taken to court for accommodating soldiers more than 100 yards from where their horses were stabled. Mr Williams explained he had only five beds in his hotel which he could not give to the military "because they were often slept in by the first gentlemen and ladies of the land." He had therefore obtained quarters for the men at the Three Horseshoes in Eden Stree, just 144 yards from the Griffin. He was fined £2 with 9s. costs.

The billeting laws were not repealed until 1921. In the meantime, Kingston suffered. On June 8, 1861 for example, the *Surrey Comet* reported that 450 men and 282 horses had been quartered in Kingston the previous week as Battalions of the Royal Artillery journeyed from Woolwich to Aldershot.

The harassment was summed up by the *Kingston and Surbiton News* of June 21, 1890:

> "When a party of soldiers comes into the town the men are armed with a ticket denoting the public house at which they are to be put up for the night. With this in his possession, no landlord dare refuse the holder shelter, although generally speaking he is a very unwelcome visitor and the few pence which the Government offer in return for a night's lodging and food do not at all recoup the landlord for the expense incurred. Licensed victuallers have to put up with many inconveniences, and not the least of them is the imperative necessity of throwing open their houses to the military whenever they happen to come, which in Kingston is pretty frequently."

The paper reported that on the previous Friday a detachment of more than 100 men from the Royal Horse Artillery had arrived in town. On Tuesday 115 men with 184 horses belonging to the Army Service Corps had rode in from Woolwich. The result was booted and spurred men all over the place, galloping their horses and generally intimidating road users. These men had left on Wednesday, only to return on Thursday on their way back to London.

Vagrants and "tourists" were an even greater problem on the streets. Thousands came to Kingston because it was the centre of the Poor Law Union, or because of its proximity to several race courses. Others made a halt in the town because it was convenient for the road to the South Coast, Portsmouth, Guildford and other key centres. Many relied for shelter on the pubs and squalid lodging houses, several of which were centred on the infamous Back Lanes area. For instance, on February 12, 1881 the *Surrey Comet* reported that 49,653 people had been accommodated in the town's common lodging houses during the previous 12 months.

The rest looked to the "palace on the hill', as the workhouse was often called. Reporting on tramps and vagrancy in Kingston Union, the *Surrey Comet* of November, 1881 said that from Michaelmas 1872 to 1881, no fewer than 101,593 tramps had been given bed and board at

Kingston Workhouse. In 1873 the total for the year had been 5,405. In the first ten months of 1881 it had been 15,705.

"Some 500 a week are provided with bath, supper, bed and breakfast," remarked the *Surrey Comet,* adding that an "authoratative estimate" had shown that only 10% of casuals were genuinely seeking work. The other 90% were professional beggars.

Many were said to be people of the most depraved kind.

> "A student of human faces would be appalled at the variations of evil he would find stamped upon the countenances of those, male and female, who nightly claim a bed in the casual ward," declared Mr J.H.W. Sumner at a meeting of Kingston Board of Guardians in June 1880. "Every foul passion of the human heart has transfigured the face with hideous ferocity and in 99 cases out of every 100 the faces tell of a life of vicious indulgence. All traces of anything like divine creation has disappeared. The face is wolfish, bestial, devilish."

That same month a townsman had written to the Comet to complain that from 5 p.m. each day Coombe Road, from the railway arch to the corner of Gloucester Road, was filled with droves of male and female tramps, "awaiting the time to be admitted to those nice, clean, much too comfortable beds and baths." These tramps, he said, lay on the bank and across the road, spitting, smoking and swearing. People who wished to get to Norbiton Station had to use Manorgate Road instead.

Another townsman, writing in the *Surrey Comet* of January 22, 1881 complained of "able bodied tramps and beggars who infest Kingston," carrying a few matches or oranges to disarm the police.

> "Men and women follow and annoy passengers to an incredible extent, especially ladies, walking close by their side, probably with the aim of picking their pockets, or intimidating them into giving money," he wrote.

There was much support for the *Surrey Comet's* leader column of January 3, 1880 which declared that vagrancy had become a social disease and the system of workhouse relief too indulgent.

"The housing of vagrants is so far superior to that of honest labouring men that the casual ward, with its comforts of warmth, good bedding, food and cleanliness forms part of a legalised system which has the effects of encouraging idleness and professional begging which are next door to crime," it said.

Were the casual wards really so luxurious? Until 1868 vagrants were lodged in the workhouse stables. Then new wards were built, and a *Surrey Comet* reporter went to investigate. He found that would-be lodgers first had to apply for an order at the police station. Once at the workhouse (from which Kingston Hospital developed) they were given a very thorough tepid bath, supplied with nightshirts and directed to the dormitory. In the meantime their clothes were put in an oven to destroy vermin.

"It is admitted that after two or three good bakings, the articles subjected to this treatment may almost be said to have been done brown, and are not quite so durable as they were before," reported the *Surey Comet's* observer.

Next morning the 'guests' had to pay for their lodging by picking oakum if they were women or breaking a bushel of stones if they were men.

Evidently conditions became tougher in later years.

The *Kingston and Surbiton News* of August 21, 1897 published a feature by an anonymous writer describing a night in the casual wards. He told how new arrivals were given plain bread and water for supper. They had to rise at 5.30 a.m. for 8 ozs of bread with water. Then came the dreaded task of turning the pumps. Kingston Workhouse got all its water from a 60 foot well, raised by tramps and forced up a further 80 feet into tanks housed in a tower (which still survives).

"This is done by means of two cranks in the pump room at the back, each large enough for four men to turn, and these eight men only finish their days' work when the dial on the wall registered 8,000," said the writer. "Eight robust, strong young navvies will sometimes finish this modicum of penal servitude at 4 p.m. On the other hand, eight ordinary, weakly fellows will toil from 7 a.m. to 11.45 a.m., then knock off for dinner (8 ozs bread, 1½ozs of the commonest cheese, and water) on again from 1 p.m. to 6 p.m., and if the dial doesn't acquit them, on again after supper (8 ozs bread and water) till 8 o'clock.

> "If the dial still shows a deficit, then two hours more in the morning, just to loosen the limbs for the day's march to the next 'spike' (casual ward). But it's not always the pump; the entertainment is sometimes varied to threequarters of a fathom of wood being cut with a circular saw, motive power being supplied by six casuals turning a flywheel till this little slice of piecework is accomplished and the operatives are almost too tired to eat their piece of dry bread."

The reporter noted that a casual ward extension was in course of building, with 20 sets of rooms ranged ten a side down a stone corridor. Each set consisted of a 'bedroom' measuring 5ft by 8ft, furnished with a hammock and stool. Behind it was a still smaller room, containing only a hammer. With that the casuals would be compelled to break up some 1 cwt of hard flint or rock, converting it into macadam small enough to pass through the 1¼-inch squares of a grating at the back.

"Is it possible, think you, that a man can get work with the 'spike' on his hands?" asked the correspondent, telling of a young tailor who, after a stay in the Kingston wards had walked round in a state of semi-starvation for the next 10 days with work staring him in the face. The heavy hammers had so lacerated his hands that he could not hold a needle.

There was a marked decline in readers' letters to newspapers on the unparalleled comforts of the casual wards after that feature appeared.

Shopping Revolution

Glamour. That was what Kingston required as it struggled to keep pace with post-railway economy. It was something the town had never possessed. Quaintness and a certain kind of indestructible charm it had in plenty, but glamour – no.

From the mid-19th century the old town was forced, reluctantly, to do something about its looks. It had never needed to before. For at least 700 years people had come from miles around to buy goods in the Market Place and the shops around it. Most of these buildings had survived virtually unchanged for centuries. They were small, dark and plain, each supplying its own specialist lines.

Two things changed that uncomplicated state of affairs. One was the rapid migration to the area of a new and moneyed class of resident, eager to display its wealth in opulent standards of home and dress. The dim little caverns that served for shops in Kingston did little to attract here. An even more potent factor was the development in the Metropolis of new department and co-operative stores, where enticingly displayed goods in unprecedented variety were offered in smart surroundings at competitive prices. Shopping, hitherto a strictly practical necessity, took on a new dimension as a pleasurable leisure pastime. Shoppers who did not like the look of what Kingston had to offer could – and all too often did – go by train to the London emporiums instead. The *Surrey Comet* noted with anger and dismay the station platforms laden with cases and hampers of goods ordered by local customers from the new London stores. Soon the majority of richer families were buying only perishables from the shops at home.

> "The revolution which the new co-operative system has introduced into the customs of trade altogether puts out of gear the quiet, steady, easy-going habits of those respectable firms which are the commercial strength of our contry towns. It is hard to compete with the spacious and pretentious premises of the co-operative stores where, it is said, everything can be

> obtained at once and where it is often fallaciously supposed that the best of goods may be purchased infinitely cheaper than at the shops," declared the *Surrey Comet's* leader column on New Year's Day, 1881.

Kingston's shopkeepers had just experienced the gloomiest Christmas trading in memory, and it was evident that the seductive new "co-operatives" were largely to blame.

This was a middle-class movement, quite separate from the working class co-operative retailing launched in the 1840's. It began in 1864 when a group of Post Office clerks clubbed together to buy a chest of tea, saving themselves 9d. a pound. Two years later the group opened a retail shop in the Strand. First they specialised in groceries. Then they added clothing and household items. By 1870 the stock embraced almost everything required in everyday shopping and the Civil Service Stores, as it became known, was a force to be reckoned with.

Then in 1871 a group of army officers combined to buy a few cases of wine at wholesale prices. Soon they formed a society to buy other merchandise in bulk. The following year they opened a retail store in Victoria Street under the name Army and Navy. By 1887 the Army and Navy organisation had no fewer than 5,000 employees, 50,000 life members and subscribers were making more than 8,000 purchases a day.

With the *Surrey Comet* as their mouthpiece, Kingston traders raged against the "greedy insatiableness" of the big stores.

"Everything from a paper of pins to a fat goose may be obtained at these gigantic establishments," continued the New Year's leader column of 1881. "With astonishing speed the old conservative courtesies of trade have been demoralised. A levelling principle now prevails throughout all branches of commerce, and the ambitions of the modern man of business seem to be to become a jack of all trades rather than to be a master of any. Casting to the winds the oldfashioned maxim 'live and let live', so honoured among past generations of tradesmen, each shopkeeper now infringes upon the domain of every other with impunity, and with a licence that is almost a parody on freedom displays in his shop window such an incongruous medley that it is puzzling to guess to what branch of trade he professes to belong."

From angry bewilderment, Kingston's shopkeepers changed their attitude to one of jealous rivalry.

> "Grocers sell wine and whisky, so publicans sell tea and coffee. Even the most fashionable and respectable of our drapers tempt customers to buy their silks and satins by under-selling all kinds of nick-nacks foreign to their

business, such as hair brushes, Christmas cards and bon-bons. Unless they check this they will weaken their case against co-operatives and encourage their neighbours to seek reprisals," chided the *Surrey Comet.*

But no amount of chiding could halt the shopping revolution. Reluctantly, with many a sigh for the old, uncompetitive ways, Kingston began re-furbishing its shopping image. The favourite ploy was to tack a showy new frontage onto an existing old building.

"At the present rate of progress, every place of business which has a long record of years will have put on a new face," remarked the *Kingston and Surbiton News* of August 14, 1886.

This policy, adopted largely for make-do-and-mend reasons at the time, has provided modern conservationists with many a joyful discovery, and the planners with many a headache, as buildings of seemingly no historic value prove to have structures of fine antiquity hidden behind their 19th and 20th century facades.

Notable examples are 1 Thames Street, now the home of Bradford and Bingley Building Society, revealed in the 1970's to be a 16th century merchant's house, and numbers 30 and 40/44 High Street, which made headlines in 1983 by proving to be Georgian and Stuart belles hiding behind Victorian aprons.

Those years of cosmetic activity, as Kingston's shopkeepers fought to counter the lure of London, are still engrossingly evident now. Look above many of today's display windows and one will see the embellishments made in a campaign described by the local press as "putting new faces on old bodies."

Of particular interest is the "Dutch Renaissance" style, used by wine merchants Ellis and Co. when they opened at 36 Market Place in March 1889 and by Mr Henry Tyler when he glamourised his boot and shoe shop at 34 Thames Street three months later.

Both made flamboyant use of brick, stone facings and terracotta. Mr Tyler used a kind of topknot arrangement to ensure that his shop was – and still is – the most eyecatching on the east side of the road.

"The shop is a distinct ornament to the town and adds greatly to the appearance of that excellent business thoroughfare, Thames Street," remarked the *Kingston and Surbiton News.*

Ellis used swags of terracotta grapes and foliage to garnish their frontage, said by the *Kingston and Surbiton News* to be "of imposing appearance which attracts much attention."

At the same time, Mr J.J. Holland was busy extending the fashion and fabrics business he had acquired at 11 Thames Street in 1865. In 1889 he secured the recently deceased Thomas Jackson's fruit and flower shop next door and used it to enlarge his original store behind a facade so pleasing that when W.H. Smith and Sons entirely rebuilt the premises in 1981 they were obliged to go to great added trouble and expense to ensure it remaind intact.

These three fillips to Kingston's ageing looks attracted so much attention that members of the Royal family drove out incognito from White Lodge in Richmond Park to inspect them.

They were so enthusiastic in their praise of the "Dutch Renaissance" that Nuthalls elaborated on the same theme when they re-built their premises in Thames Street in 1902. The firm had been famous for its tea, confectionery and catering since the days of William IV; sadly, the business disappeared in 1933 but the exuberant frontage of their shop, restaurants and banqueting rooms, now the home of Millets, still remains as a reminder of Kingston's post-railway shopping revolution.

An even more intriguing souvenir of that revolution and of Nuthalls survives immediately opposite in the form of the little Tudor building that straddles the Thames Street/Market Place corner, and is now part of Boots. It dates from before 1590 and was solidly authentic when in 1885 Nuthalls, who ran it as The Old Segar Shoppe, decided it did not look genuine enough. They called in a Mr J.M. Duffell to make it resemble what they thought a 16th century building should have been rather than what it actually was. We can still see the results today. Charming though it is, its windows, timbering and other embellishments would amaze the original builders.

It was an example of how, when it comes to architecture, Kingston seems always to have preferred pseudo to the real thing. Another instance is the building that now houses a Berni Inn on the West side of the Market Place. For the greater part of the 19th century it was the home of the celebrated corn merchants and millers J. & B. Marsh, who removed its early Stuart front and replaced it with one in imitation Old English style.

Adjoining the former Segar Shoppe, and also owned by Boots, are premises which attract visitors from far and wide with their richly ornate frontage of carved kings, queens and gilded scrolls.

But, splendid though it is, it is not the ancient masterpiece so many imagine it to be. One section was completed in 1909, the other in 1929, and both were the idea of Alderman William Finny, who served seven terms as Mayor of Kingston. The building beneath has an unexpected history. Part of it was originally a library and bookshop owned early in the 19th century by Benton Seeley and later by Biden and Co. In 1850 it was acquired by George Phillipson, who ran it for the next 56 years.

Nothing Without Labour was his motto and he was working in the shop until a fortnight before his death in 1906.

In 1880 Mr Phillipson acquired the shop next door. He decided to rebuild the two shops as one and commissioned the noted local architect, Mr Charles Luck, to draw up designs. Edwin Wells of Eden Street carried out the demolition and re-construction but there was a disagreement and Phillipson barred Wells from the building before paying. Wells regained possession by force. Phillipson ejected him with even more force. Wells, backed by hired 'troops' again succeeded in gaining the building, watched by several hundred enthralled spectators who had gathered in the Market Place to witness the drama. Wells was brought to court in January 1882 and, after a prolonged hearing that attracted avid interest, was fined £5. At the back of the premises, abutting on the churchyard, can still be seen the deeply carved inscription, "G. Phillipson's wall."

The building, even without its later embellishments, was valuable in attracting prestigious customers to Kingston. The whole of the first-floor was a library where Queen Victoria was a regular customer and where the Emperor and Empress Frederick of Germany had standing orders.

However, the most respected pioneer in Kingston's retailing revolution was Shrubsoles. Documents now owned by the National Westminster Bank indicate that this drapery and fashion firm was founded in Kingston Market Place in 1760. Under various names and owners it has remained there ever since, and is now the oldest retail business in the Royal Borough, and one of the oldest in Britain. It was already a store of the highest social standing, favoured with the custom of Queen Victoria, when brothers John and Henry Shrubsole enlarged and re-organised it on London department store lines in 1866.

The *Surrey Comet* of April 14 described the five new showrooms "handsomely decorated and fitted without any expense being stinted to make them equal to those of first-class West End firms."

Every improvement has its price. Customers soon found that if they wanted the benefits of London style shopping and its competitive prices, they would have to relinquish such luxuries as prolonged interest-free credit. Hitherto Shrubsoles, like other stores of their class, had been accustomed to bill their distinguished patrons no more than once a year, and the richer the customer, the longer the credit. Now cash transactions were essential if firms were to remain competitive. In 1868 Shrubsole's began advertising 5% discount on purchases of £1 or more "paid in cash on the spot."

Two years later Shrubsoles engaged the eminent Decimus Burton –

architect of the triumphal arch at Hyde Park Corner. He designed them an elegant shop frontage in what the *Surrey Comet* of April 23, 1870 praised as "a style never yet before attempted in this town . . . few houses of business in town or country could be found to surpass it. The elaborate decoration occupied a considerable time in execution and visitors gazed in apparent astonishment at such artistic display in Kingston."

In 1873 the store was bought by Joseph Hide and continued under his name until 1977, when it was acquired by House of Fraser. It is ironic that it now bears the name Army and Navy – one of the pioneer "co-operatives" which sparked Kingston's shopping revolution and was once the old store's bitter rival.

Tucked away in the heart of the Army and Navy store is a fine 17th century carved oak staircase which illustrates more effectively than words how the shopping "improvements" of the 19th century were sometimes carried out with a heavy hand.

The staircase, which now takes customers to household goods on the first floor, was originally the centrepiece of the Castle Inn, which was converted into shops in the first half of the 19th century. One of the naked, cherub-like figures carved into the balusters has been cruelly mutilated. The reason is to be found in the store's archives, which record that a high-born lady customer in the 19th century was offended to find a nude, carved on the staircase. The proprietor promptly called for a knife and removed the offending portion of the cherub's anatomy. The customer was mollified. That was more important than the scarring of a unique staircase, immortalised in Jerome K. Jerome's classic, *Three Men in a Boat.*

While Shrubsoles were attending Queen Victoria and many other Royals and aristocrats, Frank Bentall was buying James Hatt's dingy little shop in the then unfashionable Clarence Street. Young Frank opened for business in 1867, serving behind the counter 13 hours a day and pioneering the policy of instant cash refunds on goods that failed to please. Like many other shops in Victorian Kingston, Bentalls expanded by acquiring adjacent properties. By 1900, when Frank had his sons George and Leonard in the business with him, Bentalls had bought four neighbouring shops. They have continued Kingston's shopping revolution ever since. Now they occupy the East side of Wood Street and have a magnificent frontage modelled on the William and Mary portion of Hampton Court Palace.

Clarence Street, which had long specialised in builders' yards, workshops, pubs and the less erudite shops, began to smarten early in the 1880's when Trigg's stonemason's yard was replaced by Bournemouth Terrace, a row of shops whose handsome neo-Georgian frontages still survive on the upper levels of what are now numbers 42-50 on the south side of the street near its junction with Eden Street.

Another improvement was provided in 1886, when Mr Smith rebuilt his old-established furniture shop on the corner of Fife Road. His building, with its distinctive corner dome still survives, and is still a furniture store.

The ousting of old shopping patterns, based on long and trusting relationships between retailers and their customers, had some unwelcome effects. They are clearly spelt out in the advertised aims of the Kingston and Neighbourhood Traders' Association, founded in 1871 as the forerunner of today's Kingston, Surbiton and New Malden Chambers of Commerce. The secretary was James Wright, the treasurer John Shrubsole, and the first advertisement announced that "this Association has been formed for the protection of tradesmen from robbery, fraud and deposition and for affording greater facilities to its members in the recovery of debts due to them at as little outlay and trouble as possible." The membership subscription was 24s. This was reduced to 10s. 6d. the following year, when the Association was said to be in "full working order" and very successful. Local shopkeepers, struggling to hold their own in the shopping revolution, had yet another unwelcome innovation to contend with when influential London companies began opening branch shops in Kingston and Surbiton. This pattern, which today has banished most of the small, native shops from the high streets of Britain, is often regarded as a 20th century development. In fact, it began in the Kingston area a century ago, and seems to have met with little enthusiasm.

"Still they come," remarked the *Kingston and Surbiton News,* wearily, on June 12, 1886. "The fashion of London tradesmen following their town customers by opening branches in the suburbs is on the increase. One of the latest instances is a well-known bootmaker in the Strand, who had taken premises at Surbiton Park Terrace."

The handsome new shop facades hid an unpleasant fact of Victorian life: the appalling conditions endured by shop workers.

The *Surrey Comet* had begun compaigning vigorously on their behalf in 1858, when thousands of building workers had organised a national strike.

> "It is strange that while big, brawny men of healthy outdoor occupation are striking for a nine-hour day, we should have to plead the cause of a class considered above them in the social scale who toil indoors with wan faces and weary limbs for 14, 16 and sometimes even 18 hours a day," declared the leader column of September 17. "From 6.30 in the morning

until 10 and 11 at night many people in Kingston drudge on.
A 14 or 16 hour day is normal here."

The paper pointed out the "disease, premature death and moral evil" caused by such working hours, and praised three local drapers who had set an example by closing at the early time of 8 p.m. during the winter. Readers were exhorted never to shop after 7 p.m. in winter and 8 p.m. the rest of the year. The *Surrey Comet* also asked employers who paid weekly to give out wages on Thursdays, and so reduce late night trading (often until midnight) on Saturdays.

At first the campaign bore fruit. The *Surrey Comet* of October 20, 1860, carried an advertisement announcing that the traders of Kingston had agreed to close their shops at 8 p.m. from November 1 to June 1. Evidently this concession was short-lived. In September 1875 the *Surrey Comet* was complaining that while mechanics were getting more and more free time shop people, including journeymen, needle-women, dressmakers and milliners, as well as counter assistants, were working longer and longer.

The following September it published a letter from a shop assistant who described himself and his colleagues as "the white slaves of Kingston", toiling 15 hours a day, six days a week, with only one hour off. Labourers and artisans, he said, now worked ten hours a day, and bank clerks only six.

Not until the summer of 1881 did the suffering shopworkers achieve what to them was a half-holiday when the principal traders of Kingston agreed to close at 5 p.m. each Wednesday.

They did so only after being called to a meeting chaired by the Vicar, the Revd A.S.W. Young. Later the grateful "white slaves" thanked Mr Young with an illuminated address.

Earning a Living

Malting and brewing with their allied trade of inn-keeping were for centuries the staples of Kingston's economy. At the start of the Victorian era, Kingston had four main breweries, several small ones and a host of flourishing malthouses. At its end, only one brewery remained and all the malthouses had closed.

A Government commission, set up to study the municipal corporations in England and Wales, published its report on Kingston in January 1834. The report states, "the principal trade of Kingston consists in malt. There are 11 malthouses in the immediate vincinity of the town."

Frederick Merryweather confirmed the importance of the malting industry.

"In 1837 . . . there were a dozen opulent maltsters and 38 goodly malthouses in the town," he wrote in his *Half a Century of Kingston History,* published in 1887.

Alderman Frederick Gould, who served two terms as Mayor and was one of the most forceful personalities ever to serve on Kingston Council, recalled the scene when he first arrived in Kingston from his native Bath in 1839:

"There were malthouses visible in all directions, and everywhere one turned there were Inland Revenue officers," he told the *Surrey Comet* in an interview published in the Royal Diamond Jubilee issue of June 1897. "Many of the maltsters at that time were credited with having made large fortunes by evading the revenue officers. There was a famous firm in Hampton Wick – Messrs Tooth – who shipped large quantities of malt to Australia . . . the old maltmen, many of whom were wealthy men, were to be seen about the streets in their skullcaps, knee breeches and worsted stockings, and every day they did their full share of hard work by the side of their men."

Alderman Gould mentions that major malthouses were in the High Street, the Bittoms, Surbiton Road and the Back Lanes – the labyrinth of courts and alleys that lay between Wood Street and the riverside until the 1890's. George Ayliffe, in his published recollections of Kingston in 1837, named other maltings in London Road, Clarence Street and on the east side of the junction where Union Street and Eden Street meet.

Much of the barley needed for malting was grown in and around Kingston. On arrival at the malthouse, the grain was steeped in water for two days, then spread over the malting floor. There it remained for some days, frequently combed through with special rakes. During this time the barley heated up, prompting germination. Rootlets grew, causing the starch in the grain to turn sugary. The barley was then picked up with special wood or tin shovels and loaded into kilns, where heat from funnels below percolated through the grain, making it hard and dry. Finally, the grain was sifted to remove the rootlets which, with the husk, were used for animal feed.

It was a process requiring great expertise. The floor temperature, the sugar content of the grain and many other physical factors were of key importance to the flavour and quality of the finished product before it was despatched downstream to London on barges. These vessels returned to Kingston laden with coal, shipped into London from South Wales and the north.

The pagoda-shaped roofs of the malthouses had been familiar features of the town since time immemorial. Then, with brutal speed, they ceased to be reassuring symbols of Kingston's prosperity and became instead symbols of ruin. Their demise occurred in the months following the opening of the railway station at Surbiton in 1838.

"The river had given facilities to the Kingston maltsters which the inland traders of Surrey could not possess; but now the rail took the malt from distant towns to the London market at lower rates then the bargemasters. The diminution of trade was so great that in the spring of 1840 there were 17 large malthouses vacant in the town," records Frederick Merryweather.

A few tenacious spirits kept malting alive in Kingston, albeit with ever-decreasing strength, until the end of the century. *Kelly's Directory* for 1884 lists four maltsters in Kingston: Lascelles Tickner and Co., who had taken the maltings run for so long by the indomitable Wadbrook family in Surbiton Road; D. Jupp in Brighton Road, Hodgson Brothers in High Street and Henry Paice in Eden Street. In the Directory for 1899 Lascelles Tickner have been replaced by the Liddell Engineering Co., D. Jupp had become a carman and coal merchant and Hodgson's malthouse in High Street has become Smelt's furniture shop. Only Henry Paice remains as the last independent maltster in the Royal Borough. His premises were at 45 Eden Street, on a site now covered by Eden Walk. In fact, all of Kingston's malthouse buildings have been lost to public memory, save for one notable exception.

In 1895 William Smelt, owner of antique furniture showrooms in Esher and Molesey, bought Hodgson Brothers' malthouses in Kingston High Street and at once replaced the frontage with a pseudo-ancient one of his own design. Kingstonians, who have always tended to value their reproduction buildings more highly than their genuine period ones, loved Mr Smelt's creation from the moment it opened for business on December 11.

"Stucco work and solid oak beams and cross ties with red brick supporting columns have blended to produce a capital effect, while an oak-covered shield, having the inscription "Old Malthouse, 1617' bears witness to the antiquity of the greater part of the building," declared the *Kingston and Surbiton News* of December 7, 1895, adding that pillars and beams inside the three-floored premises had been 'stained and carved in imitation of the antique.'

For the next 70 years the building attracted tourists, photograpers and postcard artists. Its conspicuous kiln top, a unique feature from malting days, gave special character to the street scene.

In 1965 it was given the protection of a Building Preservation Order. On a Sunday morning, six weeks later, it was illegaly demolished. Now Kingston's last remaining malthouse, still regretted by many local residents, has been replaced by an office block.

Of Kingston's many breweries in the 19th century, four took pride of place: Hodgson's, Nightingale's, Fricker's and East's. Hodgson's was the oldest, the largest and the one that surived longest. It occupied an extensive site in Brook Street and, though the company's surviving records did not date back beyond 1760, was commonly believed to have been in operation for well over 300 years when brewing finally ceased in 1951.

During the first half of the 19th century the business was owned by the Rowlls family. They occupied Kingston Hall, a Georgian mansion which stood in beautiful grounds adjoining the brewery. In 1854 Charles Rowlls sold the brewery to William Hodgson who, according to an article in the *Sunday Citizen* of November 18, 1882 had arrived in London with only a sovereign in his pocket. Through hard work, he gathered enough to acquire Rowlls' brewery, together with some 90 tied freehold and leasehold public houses. Under his charge the business, which had been static, increased by leaps and bounds. After William Hodgson's death in 1875, the brewery passed to his sons, William Sanford Hodgson and Charles Durant Hodgson. William Sanford, according to the *Sunday Citizen,* threw himself into the business and mastered every detail. But he and his brother never agreed and eventually were not on speaking terms. This led to the takeover of the business by a limited liability company in October, 1886. The cause of the feud was said to have been partly political. William Sanford was chairman of the local Primrose Conservative party. His brother was a vociferous radical candidate, and as such was constantly mauled by the local Press.

The newly-formed company, under the name of Hodgson's Kingston Brewery, proved prosperous. A feature in the *Surrey Comet* of April 17, 1901, describes total output in 1887 as 29,000 barrels with a declared dividend of 6½%. By 1900 output had risen to 40,700 and the company owned 130 tied houses.

The brewery occupied most of the west side of Brook Street and comprised its own draymaking, farriers', coopers', blacksmiths' and wheelwrights' shops, together with a malthouse. By then the hops were said to be selected from the best Kentish crops. In pre-railway days they would probably have been picked from an abundance of local crops grown in and around Kingston, particularly on what are now the residential estates of Spring Grove and Southborough.

Volume 4 of the *Victoria County History of Surrey,* published in 1905, describes Hodgson's as "one of the oldest breweries in England and one of the largest and most important in the country", employing 74 workers.

When it was acquired by Courage in 1943 it was producing 2,500 casks a week. But in 1951, with the growing popularity of bottled beer, brewing ceased in Kingston and the premises were given over to bottling. In 1965 the building was closed for good. It lay derelict until 1971, when it was severely damaged by fire. Now the site is covered by a multi-storey block of offices, car park and shops and the only surviving fragment of Hodgson's Kingston Brewery is the stable block which, converted into workshops, still stands at the junction of Brook Street and Penrhyn Road.

Fricker's Eagle Brewery was a handsome riverside building situated on the Eagle Wharf in Kingston High Street. It was established by Thomas Fricker in the early 19th century and subsequently passed to his son, Arthur. Arthur died suddenly in 1876 at the early age of 37, and the business was continued under trustees during the minority of his children. In 1903 it was advertised for sale. Great efforts were made by the Fricker family to retain possession and avoid the sale, and they took the matter to the Court of Chancery. To no avail. The building, described in the sale advertisements as "a modern half-tower 15 quarter brewery with goodwill of more than 7,500 barrels per year", was sold on May 16 together with its 38 tied houses. Representatives from all the leading British breweries gathered for the sale, but none could match the then record sum of £121,280 paid by Hodgsons to buy out their local brewery.

Hodgsons continued to operate the Eagle Brewery for a few years, but their main interest was the acquisition of Fricker's tied houses. Brewing on the site ceased and the wharf was used by coal barges instead. The brewery building has disappeared, but frontage of the Eagle Tap, where customers quaffed Fricker's Family Ale (nine shillings for nine gallons) or the Superior Beer (15 shillings for nine gallons) has been preserved in the High Street. Most of the former Fricker pubs also survive, including the nearby Ram, the Albion on the Fairfield and the Richmond Park Hotel in Kings Road.

George Nightingale established his Kingston Brewery in about 1830. It was on the north side of what was then Pheasant Lane, but is now called Vicarage Road, and had another frontage onto Water Lane. Early in the 1860's Mr Nightingale built a new brewery on the opposite side of the lane. It was equipped with the latest steam-driven plant and became celebrated among connoisseurs as Nightingale's Steam Brewery. It was specially noted for Sovereign Ale, which won international awards.

George Nightingale took a prominent part in local affairs and was Mayor of Kingston in 1846. He was joined in the business by his nephew, Stephen. After George Nightingale's death another nephew went into partnership with Stephen. But soon after Stephen's death late in the 1880's the business ceased. The sale advertisements of April 1891 refer to a brewery fitted with six-quarter steam plant. They also state that the proprietor has retired from a business that has been in the family "for over 60 years."

The premises were bought by Kingston Corporation and demolished to make way for the town's first council-built housing. Today the site is about to be used for a new road and department store; but Nightingale's four pubs still survive under different owners. They are the Six Bells in Albert Road, the Grey Horse in Richmond Road, the Jolly Brewers in Canbury Passage and the Castle in King Charles Road, Surbiton.

The fourth brewery was owned by Kingston's first non-conformist Mayor, Joseph East. In 1846 he came to Kingston from his native Berkshire and soon made his mark on the town and on a little Tudor brewery in Church Street, then being run as Flint and Shaw. He became a partner, the name of the business changing to Flint and East. By the

1850's he had acquired full ownership and Joseph East's Albion and Star Brewery, as it became known, acquired several pubs. Joseph East continued to run the Church Street premises as a brewery and tap until 1867. Then he moved to new, purpose-built premises in Oil Mill Lane (now Villiers Road). Meanwhile his old premises, after three-and-a-half centuries as a brewery and inn, became shops, known today as numbers 6, 6a and 8 Church Street.

Shortly before Joseph East's death in 1891, his Oil Mill Lane premises were bought by Charringtons. However, they never brewed there and ultimately the brewery became the VP winery, which still occupies the greatly extended site today.

Surbiton also boasted two breweries. One was the Surbiton Hill Brewery in Alpha Road. The other was the Lamb Brewery in Brighton Road.

In 1856 the ower of the Surbiton Hill Brewery was a Mr H.W. Vachell, who advertised in the *Surrey Comet* to deny rumours that his fine ales and beers were in fact made by another firm. In later years advertisements refer to "Henry Cooper junior's Surbiton Hill Brewery." In March 1885 the premises were advertised for sale as "a five-quarter plant with private residence, brewhouse, stores, stables, cart shed and large yard, together with taphouse adjoining."

There is no further mention of the brewery, and street directories indicate that its site was re-developed as housing.

The Lamb Brewery survived until the 1890's. Today it is remembered in the name of the Lamb public house.

Kingston's long alliance with alcohol included spirits. There was a distillery south of Bishop's Hall Lane, off Thames Street, from the late 18th to the mid-19th century, latterly occupied by the Nicholas family.

Rating assessments also show another distillery in the area of West-by-Thames – the former name of the High Street. This was in the hands of the Stevens family for most of the 18th century and into the early years of the 19th, and may have been the same business that survived alongside the Creek and Clattern Bridge until 1925. Street directories indicate that from about 1850 this distillery was being run by Robert Horne, a former maltster in Hampton Wick and Kingston. Robert Horne died in 1882, whereupon his distillery was bought by Alexander Addington. In 1886 the business was acquired by its former manager, Edward Coppinger, who had arrived from his native Kent eight years previously, and was elected mayor of Kingston in 1890. He retained the business until his retirement in 1919, when he sold out to Messrs Searle Gordon and Company

Kingston Distillery ceased operations in 1925, and was auctioned by Nightingale Page and Bennett on March 25. Advertisements at that time described it as "a well-equipped rectifying and compounding gin distillery, enjoying the distinction of being the only rectifier's licence south of the Thames." The auction also included Creek House, Mr Coppinger's fine Georgian residence adjoining the distillery building.

It was a sad day for Mr F.W. Barnes, who had joined the firm as a van boy in the 1860's and rose to the rank of manager and stillman. In the *Surrey Comet* of March 28, 1925 he said the firm was established in 1790 – a date proudly displayed on the distillery frontage – and that the same secret recipe for the celebrated Kingston Gin had been used throughout its existence.

Cordials were also made by the firm and, said Mr Barnes, port wine was bottled in the cellars beneath what is now the Army and Navy store on the West side of the Market Place.

The distillery and Creek House were bought for conversion into shops. Today the site is occupied by Kingston Police Station.

Kingston's preoccupation with liquor was a stimulus to the temperance movement, which in turn made the local industry in mineral waters especially lucrative.

The art of producing effervescing drinks by dissolving carbonic acid in water under heavy pressure was still relatively new when Kingston's pioneer in this field set up his "manufactory for mineral waters and effervescing beverages" in South Lane in the early 1850's. He was Thomas Raynsford, and by 1856 his advertised lines included "aerated crystal soda water, aerated potassium or magnesium waters, effervescing raspberry champagne and Jamaica ginger beer." He seems to have had local markets to himself for several years. In 1872, for example, his business is described in newspaper advertisements as "the only mineral water manufactory in Kingston. Established over 20 years." But by 1884 there was competition in the form of W. Street, who was advertising "lemonade, ginger beer and aerated water of all kinds" made at his Garfield Works in Ashdown Road. Raynsfords by this time were installed in a modern factory on the banks of the Hogsmill stream in St James's Road. In 1885, following the death of Thomas Raynsford, the business was bought by the noted dyer and dry-cleaner, Robert Harding. Two years later he sold it to a relative, Charles Durham, who ran it under the name of Raynsford until his bankruptcy in 1893. In March 1894 Raynsford's "three-floor warehouse factory with stabling for six horses in the yard and a nine-roomed house with offices attached" was auctioned at the Griffin Hotel. It was a sad moment. The Raynsford label, with its picture of the drinking fountain that is still a feature of

Kingston Market Place today, had become a familiar part of domestic life and the firm had been described in the local commercial directory of 1891 as "almost the oldest" soda water manufacturers in the country.

Raynsford's premises were acquired by John Austin and converted into a jam and preserved fruit factory. Mr Austin had been making jam and experimenting with the canning and bottling of fruit behind his shop at 44 and 46 Clarence Street for more than a decade. In proper factory conditions, Austin's jam became an important local industry and in 1913 the firm moved to prestigious new premises built to their own specifications in Cromwell Road.

Those premises still survive. They were bought by Bentalls in 1933 and have since been used as a soft furnishings factory. But the building is still called "the jam factory" by Bentall personnel.

Where Raynsford's had led, others followed. By the end of the century the many firms making soft drinks in Kingston included R. White and Son, whose factory in Fife Road is now part of Bentall's receiving dock; Clayton Bros. whose works at 2 Acre Road were specially noted for ginger beer; and the Direct Supply Aerated Water Co., whose factory in Manorgate Road, Kingston Hill has been replaced by an office block.

The temperance movement in Kingston, to whom these firms owed so much, had too long and varied a career to recount here in any detail. However, one of its ventures was of special interest. It is converted to shops now, but in 1880 it was the Leopold Coffee Tavern and could boast close links with Queen Victoria's youngest son.

The Kingston-on-Thames Coffee Tavern Co. Ltd was registered on April 12, 1880 with a capital of £1,000. Its directors included Wilberforce and Theodore Bryant, of the famous Bryant and May match firm, both of whom lived in Surbiton and were noted teetotallers. Even more influential backing for the new company came the following month, when Prince Leopold Queen Victoria's youngest son, became interested in the project, invested in a hundred shares and agreed to give his name to the building.

The aim of the Coffee Tavern Co. was to set up houses which would offer all the comforts of a well-run pub – except intoxicants.

"It is confidently expected that under judicious management they will prove a powerful agency in promoting the growth of temperance and become popular with the working classes," declared an advertisement in the Surrey Comet of April 24, 1880. "From the experience of similar companies in other places, it is believed that the shareholders may expect a fair return upon the capital invested."

It was not to be. In April 1882 the Leopold Coffee Tavern was sold as "a large hall and assembly rooms seating 30, noble bar, coffee and smoking rooms. Shop and premises adjoining let to the Singer Sewing Machine Co." Three months later the Kingston-on-Thames Coffee Tavern Co. was dissolved. The Leopold Tavern at the junction of Thames Street and Clarence Street has long been converted into shops, but is now scheduled for re-development.

Coffee taverns were a failure in New Malden also, but in Surbiton they were a success. The Anchor in Ewell Road and the Spread Eagle in Brighton Road were two particularly noted ones established by the tireless Bryant brothers.

Certainly Kingston was over-endowed with pubs of the more conventional sort. In January 1904, Kingston Temperance Union demanded a reduction in licences. Several pubs had closed down in the previous decade, yet the Union could still report that, starting from Knights' beer house near Kingston Station, they had passed 10 licensed houses in four-and-a-half minutes. Starting at a brisk pace from the Blue Anchor in Thames Street (now converted into a shop at number 10) they passed 17 pubs in eight minutes.

The same week the Association for the Promotion of Public Morality was complaining to Kingston Council that the Royal Borough overall had one licensed house per 315 of the population, while in central Kingston there was one pub to every 147 people.

The Kingston-on-Thames Coffee Tavern Co., even with Royal backing, had been no match for such competition.

* * * * * * * * *

Corn milling was an important local industry for several hundred years. The Doomsday Survey credits Kingston with five mills. By the beginning of the 19th century, though the town had three mills on the Hogsmill river, only one was used for corn. The other two had already been adapted to meet the changing industrial and social demands that dominated the century.

Chapel Mill, sometimes known as Leatherhead Mill, appears century after century in the borough archives. It stood to the east of what is now Villiers Road, and had belonged to the Lovekyn Chapel. Apparently it was converted into an oil mill in the latter half of the 18th century – possibly in 1776, when document KP/2/17 in the borough archives shows it was leased to Stephen Wedge, an oilman from Battersea. Presumably this was also the time when Oil Mill House, the beautiful Georgian residence which still stands in Villiers Road, was built for the owner of this lucrative new local industry.

For many mid-Victorian years, the mill was tenanted by Thomas Boorman who, in the words of William Drewett, "amassed a fortune there before the Free Trade movement opened up English markets free to foreign competition."

The manuscript reminiscences of Mr Bryan, compiled in 1932 and preserved in Kingston Heritage Centre, include vivid glimpses of the Oil Mill, as it was re-named, where previous generations of his family had worked.

Linseed was brought up the Thames in barges, unloaded at the public wharf at the top of Kingston High Street, then taken to the mill on horse-drawn carts. As the industry became mechanised, it was a profound difference to this isolated area with its heavy clay pastures, where town butchers grazed their cattle, and the wild hill down which huntsmen in scarlet coats raced behind their hounds. Mr Bryan records that in the mid-19th century a steam engine was installed in the mill, and the rural peace was shattered by the incessant noise of the giant "stompers" smiting the seed to extract its golden oil. It was a sound that never ceased, from midnight Sunday to midnight the following Saturday. All the men worked a 12-hour shift from 6 a.m. to 6 p.m. The night shift ended at midnight on Saturday to start again as the day shift on Monday morning.

The new night shift began at midnight on Sunday, the engineer going in two hours earlier to stoke up the fire. Bank Holidays were not initiated until 1871. Before then the men's only holidays were Christmas Day and the annual beanfeast.

Hawks Road in the 1860's had houses on its northern side only. Mr Bryan, whose family was long associated with the Oil Mill, mentions how residents lay sleepless in their beds as the noise of the stompers carried across the fields. Later, to their relief, silent hydraulic presses were installed to extract the oil. This was then transported to London in barrels borne on two-horse vans, to be used in the manufacture of paints, varnishes, printing inks, linoleum and oilcloth. The residue of linseed was made into slabs of cattle cake for delivery to the farms surrounding Kingston.

Early in the 1880's, the mill and its land were bought by the London and South Western Railway Company for a proposed line between Surbiton and Kingston. The line never materialised, and the mill and its machinery remained silent for the next 15 years. Then it was bought from the railway company by William Smith, who converted it into a factory for his famous Kingston Candles.

For nearly a century, candles had been supplied to much of Britain from an ancient shop adjoining the Castle Inn in Kingston Market

Place. It was described on the Kingston and Surbiton News of April 30th, 1887:

"... the candle shop wore to the last a sombre hue, almost black, against which the tier upon tier of snowy white dips, strung upon rods, shone out with startling brilliancy,"

The business had been started in 1762 by Robert Ranyard, who was succeeded in turn by his son, William, and grandson, Samuel. There was great demand for their goods at a time when gas and electric lighting were unknown, and Kingston's street lighting consisted of candles, set in lanterns, and lit each night by a lamplighter who went his rounds with a ladder on his shoulder. Only the wealthy could afford beeswax candles. The rest of the population used the rushlights and tallow dips that were a Ranyard speciality.

Behind their shop were gardens, extending to the creek and the river.

Here the Ranyards built their workshops and made their candles. It was a picturesque craft, virtually unchanged since Roman times; but it had a less attractive side. Tallow was made by melting down animal fat, resulting in what diarist John Evelyn described as "horrid stinks, nidirous and unwholesome smells."

When it came to "horrid stinks", there was nowhere to outdo Kingston Market Place in the 19th century. On the one hand was the Ranyard works, daily melting down the hard fats from offal and mutton. A few yards away, off Thames Street, was Kingston Tannery.

Ranyard's Kingston Tallows consisted of cotton wick, dipped repeatedly into vats of molten fat until they were of the required thickness. Like all candles of the period, they became choked with their own debris as they burned, and had to be snuffed with a special instrument every half-hour. This meant that a specially appointed candle snuffer was essential in churches, theatres and other public places. This job became redundant when Ranyards eventually produced a patent moulded candle with a specially twisted wick that needed no snuffing. Ranyard's rushlights were made from the rushes that grew in such abundance on Kingston's river banks and aits. They were peeled, bleached and dried, then dipped in scalding grease. The best were more than two feet long and burned for nearly an hour.

In 1857 Samual Ranyard retired from his business and his home over the shop. The retail side was taken by his manager, James Smith, a former farmer's lad from Northamptonshire. Smith bought the first house to be built in Kingston's newly-constructed St James's Road, and set up his candle shop there. Later he bought out Ruff's candle factory at Hampton and produced a candle that became famous nationally. This was the Kingston Sperm Candle, made from oil taken from the head cavity of the sperm whale; but it was his son, William, who transformed the firm into a major enterprise.

First he acquired the old established candle factory in Staines. By 1895 business had so increased that he bought the old Kingston Oil Mill. Here he was producing 40 tons of candles a week by 1901. His staple ingredient was paraffin wax, imported in flat cakes from Burmah and America and refined at Smith's Kingston mill by machinery powered by water from the Hogsmill.

One might have thought that by the end of the century, with gas and electricity well established, demand for candles would have slumped. However, a *Surrey Comet* reporter who visited Smith's Kingston factory in 1901 found it was not so.

"The chief demand for smaller candles is from the poorer parts of London, where they are retailed at three or four a penny," he wrote on December 11, 1901. ". . . the working classes are the main support of the industry, and the reason is not far to seek. Candles nowadays give the minimum trouble and are very cheap. Besides the domestic candle there is great demand for superior makes of candles for the piano, the dining table and the drawing room."

William Smith also pioneered various kinds of toilet and kitchen soaps. His most famous was his patented creation, Kingston Volvolutum, which remained a household name until his death. Shortly afterwards, in September 1922, his Kingston factory was bought by the famous candle firm, Price's.

Today Kingston Corporation's refuse depot occupies the site of the former Chapel Mill.

South of the Fairfield the name of Mill Street indicates that this was once the route to Middle Mill. Just when this mill was established is obscure, but there is a will in the borough archives (KB 33/1) that shows it to have been in operation some 300 years ago. By the 19th century, it had ceased flour production and embarked on a new career as a cocoa fibre factory, where the coarse fibres taken from the outer shells of coconuts were made into mats and brushes.

In the tithe apportionment of 1842, both this mill and its near neighbour, the Oil Mill, are owned by Joshua Lockwood. In July 1872, following Lockwood's death, the premises were sold by his trustees as "a compact brick-built mill called Middle Mill with a comfortable dwelling house, numerous outbuildings and rich meadow land, 11 acres total. Let to Messrs Hardcastle and Wilson, Cocoa Fibre Manufactory, on lease 20 years unexpired, £90 a year."

Save for a fire in the summer of 1865, when prepared fibre laid in for the winter months was destroyed, the cocoa fibre works attracted little publicity. However, it invested in modest advertising in the *Surrey Comet* during March, 1877, proclaiming itself to be "The Patent Cocoa Fibre Co. Ltd – the only cocoa nut fibre manufactory in Surrey. All descriptions of mats in cocoa nut fibre, plain, wool banded and all wool banded and all wool, in stock and made to order wholesale. Brushes. Cocoa nut fibre refuse for garden purposes. Fetched from mill in carts or vans at 4d. bushell. Sent to all parts of the kingdom by rail, in bags or by truck."

In 1880 the firm ceased production and the property was offered for auction at the Griffin Hotel on May 20th. Sale advertisements described it as "The Middle Mill, with water and steam power, a comfortable residence and substantially erected brick and slate mill buildings, workshop, engine house and stabling, comprising about 10 acres in all." The equipment was said to include "a powerful water wheel, 14 h.p. engine with gear, 11 carding machines, devilling, spinning and other machines.

The auction failed to find a buyer. The mill was sold privately three months later to the printers and publishers, Kelly and Co. Kelly's Mill was a valuable source of employment in the town until 1932, when the firm moved to Andover. The Kingston site was split between other concerns and Middle Mill as a self-contained community with its own workers' houses, ceased to exist. Now only the names of two pubs, the Coconut in Mill Street and the Kelly Arms in Alfred Road, survive as reminders of how people in this area once earned their living.

The third mill on the Hogsmill river in 19th century Kingston was Hog's Mill. It was reputed to have been named originally after a 12th century miller called Hog, though during the 19th century it was usually given the name of its current occupant. Thus in the 1830's and '40's it was known as Mercer's Mill, after its owner and occupier, William Mercer. By th early '50's, when he had leased it to Thomas and John Leonard, it was called Leonard's Mill. From the early '70's, when Messrs J. & B. Marsh took the tenancy, it was Marsh's Mill.

Marsh had become a familiar name in the town in 1814, when a quiet, retiring Quaker named John Marsh opened a corn chandler's business in Kingston Market Place. His shop adjoining The Griffin was an old building, formerly used to quarter troops. In due course the business passed to Mr Marsh's nephews, Joseph and Bedford Marsh, and from that time it expanded to become one of the most successful firms of its kind in the country.

The Market Place premises – now Berni's Inn – remained the headquarters, but the Marsh brothers established other depots in

Wimbledon and Esher, and also established their own mill. For several years they occupied the famous windmill, which still survives on Wimbledon Common. In fact, they were the last to work it. When they left in 1865, after a dispute with their landlord, Lord Spencer, they prudently took the stones and machinery with them to avoid competition. Then they moved into the new mill they had built in Kingston. It was in what is now called Vicarage Road and had been the site of Nightingale's Brewery.

The *Surrey Comet* of February 18, 1865, featured a minute description of the building. It was four-storeyed, equipped to grind both barley and wheat, and boasting modern machinery powered by a 16 h.p. engine housed on the ground floor. Marsh's Down Hall Mill, and the Stan-Myln Flour that was the main product, became so noted for quality that members of the Royal family headed the list of illustrious customers. Marsh's were soon catering for such a wide area that they needed additional premises. Early in the 1870's they took over Hog's Mill from the Leonards and built up immense prestigue as corn, forage, hay and straw dealers, flour and seedmen and, later, coal merchants.

Their yellow vans, pulled by teams of splendid horses, became a familiar sight at many stately homes.

The Marsh brothers also became prominent public figures in Kingston, each serving two terms as Mayor. When they retired from the firm it went into decline. Hog's Mill went first. It was acquired by Messrs Johnston in 1896 and became the Yewsabit Mill. Then, in the centenary year of the business, Marsh's Down Hall Mill was closed and the headquarters in Kingston Market Place acquired by the corn and seed firm, Thornton and Stimpson. According to Mr Bernard Stimpson, interviewed in 1975, one or two long-standing members of staff were given permission to keep the name of Marsh alive as coal and corn dealers at 118 London Road, Kingston. Later they acquired premises at Norbiton and, according to street directories, continued trading until about 1950.

The last firm to work Hog's Mill was Johnston and Co., makers of Yewsabit. This was a paste made from five secret ingredients and advertised as the King of Metal Polishes. The firm's trademark was a drummer boy of the British Guards – an appropriate choice, considering that the War Office was the firm's biggest customer. Johnston's were unswervingly nationalistic in their marketing approach. Only English employees were eligible for the 30-strong work force at the mill and advertising followed the same philosophy.

"It is incumbent on the public that they ask for and see that they get HOME manufacture which, with hardly any exception, are of very much superior quality and finish than the commonly got up articles NOT made in England," proclaimed a typical Yewsabit advertisement in the *Kingston and Surbiton News* of October 22, 1898. "Believe us, dear reader, that the continental manufacturer grows fat on your money, chuckles, and thinks 'what FOOLS those Britons are to be sure.' "

Yewsabit's finest hour seems to have come with the Boer War, when it was said to be putting a shine on most of the British Army. By 1910, however, Johnston's and Yewsabit had vanished from Kingston. The mill lingered, unworked, until the 1930's. Then it was demolished to make way for the Coronation Swimming Baths.

* * * * * * * * *

Yewsabit's most valuable social contribution to Kingston was that it extended the job prospects open to women. Bouts of severe unemployment were, for many reasons, frequent in the 19th century. They were bad enough for men. For single or widowed women they were often disastrous, and continued to be so for the rest of the century. As Thomas Philpott pointed out in his newly-formed *Surrey Comet,* the schoolroom, the needle, the wash-tub or prostitution was the only employment open to women. This unpalatable fact had been brought home to Philpott by a case in which a widow with a large family worked over a wash-tub from dawn until midnight for a few pence a day. Desperate, she pawned a few items of customer's laundry to buy food for her children, and was subsequently sentenced to six months' hard labour. Her children, meanwhile, were despatched to the workhouse.

Appalled, Philpott used his newspaper to campaign for better jobs for women, exhorting the 102,000 women of Surrey to form an association "for providing females with remunerative employment other than the needle and the schoolroom."

Writing in October 1856 he declared: "It is a national disgrace that scarecely any employment is to be found that shall provide a respectable subsistence for an industrious female." Small wonder, he added, that there were more than 25,000 women prowling the streets of London. He appealed to Kingston firms to employ women as clerks or counter assistants, and wondered why all the drapery shops should be staffed by men.

Two months later he noted acidly that the annual county ball at Kingston's Griffin Hotel could boast a long list of peeresses as patrons.

"But no titled lady will condescend to look upon the dance of death among the skeleton work women."

Throughout the century the sad, yet unconsciously humorous message, 'woman wants washing' was stuck in the front window of many a Kingston cottage. But washing was appalling work. In Norbiton and Surbiton the 'missis' system prevailed. The 'missis' secured orders and was responsible for collection and delivery. The washing and ironing was done by her team of freelance workers, who were expected to work from 7 a.m. to 8 p.m. for an average of a shilling a day plus a half-pint of beer. They had 30 minutes for lunch. The rest of the day they stood, either at the ironing table or at the tub, up to their ankles in water and blinded by steam.

In June 1872 an unprecedented thing happened: the washerwomen of Norbiton and Surbiton went on strike. Pooling their meagre funds, they hired the town crier to parade the town on June 7 calling: "This is to give notice to all women that following the wash-tub that at 12 o'clock this day there will be a meeting opposite the Black Lion, Brighton Road to take into consideration upon what terms they shall resume work. All washerwomen are requested to attend. God Save the Queen."

The women gathered, banging pots and kettles to show their anger. It was agreed that any woman who worked for less than three shillings a day and a pint of beer should be ducked in the Thames. It was further agreed that if the working day was reduced to nine hours, the women would return forthwith.

The 'missis' representatives agreed and there was an uneasy peace; but by the end of the month the town crier had been hired again, this time to advertise a mass meeting on the Fairfield for "the women that follow the wash-tub and use the flatiron." This time, as the *Surrey Comet* reported, spectators outnumbered washerwomen. Since their earlier strike, many of them were now receiving three shillings for a ten-hour day and were not on hand to support their less fortunate colleagues. The meeting fizzled out. But, inarticulate and disorganised as the washerwomen were, their action gave courage to domestic servants in Surbiton.

In the *Surrey Comet* of June 29, 1872 they proposed striking for improved pay. They were, they said, earning between £7 and £12 a year, and out of this had to buy their working caps and print dresses. Strikes and go-slows were tried in piecemeal fashion, but were too disorganised for any positive result. However, their action did succeed in spotlighting the hardship often endured by the living-in servants of parvenu families.

Male workers, when they decided to follow suit, were more efficiently united. In July 1872 the builders' labourers of Kingston gathered at the South Western Tavern in Richmond Road for what appears to be the earliest organised union meeting to be held in Kingston; for they there and then formed themselves into a branch of the London General Builders Labourer's Union to press for a uniform pay rate of 5d. an hour instead of the 4d. and 4½d. they were receiving at that time. By October they had set their sights higher. Gathering again at the South Western Tavern, which they made their branch HQ, they resolved to join London men in fighting for 6d. an hour.

Employment for women remained a social problem throughout the 19th century, particularly for those of the so-called middle class.

William Hardman became uncomfortably aware of the fact soon after settling in Kingston.

"We are on the lookout for a governess, and a very harrowing affair it is," he wrote in a letter dated October 24, 1864. "The amount of genteel poverty it reveals to us is really terrible and we cannot help regretting that we do not want several governesses."

Various schemes were launched to ease the situation. Most failed. For example, the *Kingston and Surbiton News* of December 22, 1888 reported "yet another scheme to enable ladies to get a livelihood." This was the Lady Guide Association, established by a Miss Davis to give remunerative employment "to ladies of culture and education." The Association offered lady guides for strangers visiting London at the rates of 3d. an hour, 8s. 6d. a day, 2 guineas a week or 8 guineas a month. There was one important stipulation: the lady guides could only guide ladies!

As far as women were concerned, it is interesting to find that votes for women found favour with Kingston's leading men long before the arrival of the celebrated suffragettes. Both the *Surrey Comet* and the *Kingston and Surbiton News* gave long and detailed reports of a public meeting held at the Albany Hall on March 16, 1886 in support of a Bill, then before Parliament, for granting the parliamentary vote to "duly qualified" women.

Facts and figures were produced to show that England at that time had 700,000 women householders paying rates, while the national female workforce included 347 blacksmiths; 2,738 brickmakers and dealers; 216 carpenters and joiners; 731 carriers; 216 coachbuilders; 244 plumbers and glaziers; 1,888 artists; 731 authors, writers and journalists; 110,592 bookbinders; 25,672 shoemakers; 20,644 farmers and graziers; 64 students; 46 registered medical practitioners; 734 florists and nurserymen; 376 musicians; 1,309 photographers; 2,202 printers; 7,895 upholsterers and cabinet makers and 4,241 schoolteachers.

Many of these occupations were filled by widows who had taken over their husbands' businesses. In Kingston this happened often. The *Surrey Comet,* for example, was run successfully for many years by Mary Ann Knapp after her husband died in 1863, leaving her with nine children. Another was Maria Turner, who shouldered responsibility for the jewellery business that still survives under the family name in Surbiton to this day.

These women were evidently efficient and respected. Yet their obvious capabilities seem to have done nothing to improve public attitudes towards the status of women. Perhaps that was how they wanted it. It is ironic that once Mary Ann Knapp was at the helm, the *Surrey Comet* no longer campaigned on behalf of women, as it had done in the reign of her husband, Russell, or the paper's founder, Thomas Philpott.

Thus the passing of the Married Women's Property Act in 1882 received a dubious welcome from the Comet's leader column:

> "A married woman will now have the right to have and to dispose, by sale or will, as freely as a single woman. She will no longer be considered incapable in the eyes of the law of effecting a bargain or entering into a contract. Nevertheless, its effect will be watched with some anxiety less they tend to weaken the family tie and introduce discord which usually attends divided interests."

It was left to Kingston Total Abstinence Society to achieve what to Kingston women was a major social change.

The *Kingston and Surbiton News* of June 27, 1885 reported that the Grand Temperance Dinner, just held at the Albany Hall, was "the first public dinner in Kingston at which ladies sat down with gentlemen."

Somnus Town

A curious lethargy afflicted Kingston throughout the 19th century. It is mentioned repeatedly in newspapers, documents and books, sometimes major criticism in the Government report on Kingston Corporation, published in 1834. The result was a town years behind others of comparable size and location, often nicknamed Somnus Town.

"There are no places of public amusement in Kingston, and indeed the place is altogether more distinguished for what it has not than for what it has," noted William Biden in his *History and Antiquities of the Town of Kingston-on-Thames,* published in 1852.

Why was this so?

A wealthy townsman named John Guy revealed what he considered to be the reason during a four-day battle before a committee of the House of Lords in 1860, when Kingston and Hampton Wick were fighting over the location of the terminus station of the proposed London and South West Railway's branch line from Tiwckenham.

"A little baker and a little beershop keeper and that class of men are the Corporation of Kingston," sneered Mr Guy, who lived at Norbiton Hall and owned much valuable land in Kingston.

He had probably pinpointed the reason for the Royal Borough's notorious caution and narrow vision. The town was predominately an artisan place. Many of its leaders, like most of its population, were working people of modest education who seldom needed to stir beyond the borough boundaries. Those with money were self-made men who continued to live over their business premises and work alongside their employees, supplying and servicing a close-knit community. Literature, the arts, fine architecture and other cultural amenities were low in their priorities.

After the advent of the railway, various new leisure facilities were mooted by newcomers to the town. Most were smothered by the extraordinary indifference of the people.

"It is rarely indeed that a meeting numbering more than a hundred can be drawn together in Kingston for any object depending on general support, "lamented the *Surrey Comet* of February 10, 1866. Yet this was an area where the increase in population had been estimated at two per thousand each year, compared with less than 1½ nationally.

Certainly a purpose-built concert and assembly hall was high on the planning list when the post-railway building boom reached Kingston town centre in the 1850's. During that decade, St James's Road was cut through the former grounds of Kingston Hall to provide a new route towards Surbiton Station. One of the first buildings to go up in the new thoroughfare was St James's Hall, specially designed for the multiplicity of meetings and entertainments which, it was assumed, would be an important part of life in such a rapidly expanding community. Not so. The hall was so under-used that by 1864 it had become Wills and Cartwright's furniture warehouse. Ironically, an identical fate overtook a second St James's Hall, built next to the first in 1893. That, too, became a furniture warehouse after a few years as a concert and meeting hall, and subsequently as a cinema. The dishevelled remains of this second hall remained until 1960's as a mute reproach to Kingston's apathy in supporting local events.

"Very few entertainments in Kingston make a profit," remarked Russell Knapp in 1864, lamenting the fact that pleasure seekers preferred the expense and inconvenience of travelling to London rather than supporting programmes of a high standard organised in Kingston.

William Millais, brother of the famous artist, struggled gamely during the 1860's to bring musical culture to Kingston. The Millais family were living in Kingston by the 1830's. William Ayliffe recalls that they had a cottage in Portsmouth Road, close to the junction with Surbiton Road, on a site now occupied by the TAVR. The two sons of the family, William and John, were both highly gifted. John, born in 1829, went on to become world-famous as Sir John Everett Millais, one of England's most distinguished artists. William, born in 1828, was content to use his talents in a local and purely amateur capacity, singing in the choir of St Mark's Church, Surbiton and organising concerts of high quality in Kingston.

Sir William Hardman attended one such in December 1865, and wrote of it to his friend, Edward Holroyd:

> ". . . we went to an amateur concert at the Drill Hall at Kingston, where we were much pleased. We have some rare singers here at Kingston, among whom the chief is William Millais, the brother of the celebrated J.E. Millais and perhaps the finest amateur tenor in the Kingdom."

Sir William attended another concert at the Drill Hall in April 1866. He found it "capital", but added:

"The performance had the common fault of amateur affairs: it was too long. It commenced at eight and did not terminate until past midnight."

Then there was the annual Kingston Town Ball, held at the Griffin, and the venue since the 1850's of Royals and aristocrats. But not of Kingstonians.

"The title town ball is almost a misnomer, for although many of the townsfolk complain of the want of entertainment in the place, they are generally found exceedingly backward in coming forward to support social gatherings which have been got up in the last few years at the two leading hotels in the town," said the *Surrey Comet* of January 15, 1870. "Why it should be so we cannot imagine, but that it is so is a fact." (The other "leading hotel" refered to was The Sun, which disappeared from the Market Place in 1931, to make way for Woolworth.)

Snobbery may have been the barrier here. Sir William Hardman wrote of his visit to the Griffin Ball in February, 1866.

"I should tell you 'we' are very select here in the matter of these balls. It amuses us immensely to see the strong lines of demarcation which are drawn between the best set and those beneath them in the social scale. A secret committee decides upon the admissibility or otherwise of the numerous applicants for tickets. We are honoured by carte blanche to introduce whom we choose."

The building of military barracks in Kings Road in 1875 provided an unexpected new theatrical venue. Typical of many advertisements is one which appeared in the *Surrey Comet* of January 30, 1877: "At the Theatre Royal, New Barracks, Kingston, Amateurs of the 47th Brigade Depot in farce, tragedy and opera burlesque. Front seats 2s., pit 1s."

But these were piecemeal efforts. By the dawn of the 1880's, Kingston was still without a theatre, concert hall, public library, swimming baths or many of the other amenities established elsewhere.

The *Surrey Comet* crystallised years of disgust into its leader column of January 22, 1881:

". . . Kingston is constitutionally inclined to somnalency," it declared. "Its public men are tediously cautious and the burgesses who, like the police, ought to be the stimulators of activity rarely bid them move on in the name of progress. Kingston has scarcely as yet evolved from a condition of existence suited to the social life of half a century ago.

"For a fear of going too fast we scarcely move at all and seem content to watch our neighbours lead the van in all intelligent improvements. Had a little more public spirit animated the Corporation, and a little more enterprise inspired the burgesses, Kingston would have been a handsome and prosperous town and the wretched disfigurements which disgrace the architecture of our principal streets long have disappeared. This apathy has blighted many prospects and damped the enthusiasm of those who would have been its best friends. The few achievements in the field of progress or improvements that have been attempted have not come from the town in its representative capacity and can scarcely be said to have met with much encouragement from the burgesses."

Evidently these shafts went home. By 1882, Kingston had at last achieved a public library (a makeshift affair in a room over the furnishing warehouse in St James's Road) and a swimming bath (a floating iron structure moored in the Thames and built to such a tight budget it began to disintegrate within 12 months.)

Nevertheless, Kingston can boast three great recreational legacies from the 19th century: The Fairfield, Queen's Promenade and Canbury Gardens. They are unique and splendid features, much envied by other towns. Yet each was almost obliterated by apathy and hostility.

The idea of preserving the Fairfield as what he called a "people's park" was first mooted by John Williams in 1859, when Kingston was already showing disturbing signs of becoming the congested mass it is today. The Fairfield had previously been known as Littlefield. Despite that name, it was a great open space, considerably larger than now, with a multiplicity of owners. It had long been used for grazing and agriculture, but as early as 1834 was being nibbled away by building development.

"On the East, at a place called Fairfield, some new buildings are now in progress, and we understand that it is here that the future increase to the town will probably take place," stated a Parliamentary Commission in 1834.

John Williams was one of the few men of vision on Kingston Council in the mid-19th century. According to obituary tributes in the *Surrey Comet* of June 29 and July 6, 1872 he was born at Great Bookham in 1806 and had an early life of unspeakable suffering and toil until "subsequently released by the kind interference of a family whose name is honoured wherever known." He came to Kingston in 1851 to take control of the Griffin Hotel, which was at such a low ebb it was on the point of closure. Williams carried out extensive improvements, including the building of an assembly room, and made the place so fashionable that it even attracted Royal guests. It became known as the Royal Griffin and Williams, who advertised as "postmaster by appointment to Her Majesty", was presented at Court. Hence the Royal Arms displayed on the frontage to this day.

Williams then applied his enormous energies to town matters, being elected councillor in 1855 and alderman in 1862. He soon made enemies in the Guildhall. Some were bitterly resentful that a newcomer to the town should so swiftly make his mark. Others were offended by what his friends saw as enthusiasm and his foes as conceit.

> "Ambitious he certainly was, but it was not of an unworthy nature . . . had he received the benefit of a good education, he would have been capable of taking his place among any representative men in his class," declared the *Surrey Comet,* lamenting "all the disadvantages under which he laboured and the uphill and unequal struggle he had to fight in Kingston."

He bore these sufferings bravely. Had he not, we would have no Fairfield in Kingston today and probably no Queen's Promenade either.

Williams endeavoured to waft fresh thinking through the stuffy atmosphere of the council chamber, serving three periods as Mayor in 1858, 1859 and 1864. He saw the Fairfield project as one of especially urgent social importance, and in this he had the backing of the *Surrey Comet.*

Russell Knapp summed up the situation in his leader column of October, 1, 1859:

> "Every year the area of the town widens," he wrote. "Londoners flying for fresh air from the crowded streets of the Metropolis circumvolute with their residences and cut us off further and further from green fields. In the last eight years, 3,500 homes have been added to our numbers, a large increase in a population of under 15,000 . . . open spaces which formerly afforded ample opportunity for outdoor exercises have been bricked up. Children must either be kept at home in irksome and unnatural restriction, injurious to their health, or be racing about the streets to their moral deterioration, at once a nuisance in the way of business and a source of irritation to the police."

Williams raised the matter in council, and an advertisement appeared on the front page of the *Surrey Comet* that October, "that it is desirable to enclose the Fairfield as a recreation ground for the people" and inviting subscriptions.

It was hoped to secure the entire remaining portion of the Fairfield, but the west side proved so expensive that the specially formed committee decided to settle for 15 acres instead, available for £56 a year on a long lease.

It was not to be. The hostile obstinancy of Alderman Frederick Gould and his supporters, together with the inertia of the townspeople, caused the scheme to grind to a halt. Williams took a second year's office as Mayor in a bid to steer the plan through. Still no progress.

"Differences arose and a most bitter feeling was engendered, which was perpetuated for three of four years, culminating in 1864, when he was nominated Mayor for the third time," relates the *Surrey Comet* obituary. "Ald Gould opposed the nomination with such asperity as went far to detract from the honour which should have attached to the occasion."

Nevertheless, Williams' dogged perseverance bore some fruit in 1864, when the Improvement Committee was instructed to proceed with the Fairfield scheme in a reduced form. Only 12 acres of the hoped-for 15 were ordered to be fenced off as a people's park.

Russell Knapp devoted his leader column to this decision on October 8, 1864:

"One open spot will thus be saved in the centre of the town, and we have no doubt will in a few years be all that is left of the Fairfield, for there is ominous talk of new roads and building frontages and greatly increased values, which are very beneficial to assessment for rating, but are sad destroyers of green fields and pleasant country lanes," he wrote. "Kingston is rapidly losing all traces of a rural character and acquiring the uniform appearance of a London suburb, with houses of imposing appearance, and gardens carried out with as much liberality as ham sandwiches at a charity fête, but dexterously contrived so that all should come together in the rear of the residences like a Pope John board on a large scale, enabling your neighbour to enjoy your little piece of ground almost as much as he can his own, or from his back windows to take in the whole at a glance after the manner of a governor of a local prison. Let us be thankful therefore for these 12 acres . . . we may be sure that at the rate Kingston is increasing, in a few years there will be no pleasant meadows to be reached under a mile walk from the Market Place."

Still public indifference and council hostility to the scheme continued. Appeals for subscriptions met with such scant response that when the Fairfield was at last enclosed in 1865 Williams met most of the cost from his own pocket. It amounted to some £600 for iron fencing made by the two town foundries, Stephen Harris in High Street, whose site is now occupied by the Forge House office block, and Priest and Woolnough, whose premises in Wood Street are now part of Bentalls.

Williams got no gratitude. His council foes, led by the arch-egotist Gould, so vilified him that he was obliged to avoid the council chamber altogether. When his last term of mayoral office ended, he was even denied the customary vote of thanks, Gould having let it be known that if such a vote was put he would ensure its amendment.

"So it was that he had to discharge public duties under no ordinary difficulty, and the remembrance of unrelenting opposition displayed was never effaced from his memory," remarked the *Surrey Comet.*

The type of relentless malice Gould inflicted on those he did not like is illustrated by a leaflet, dated October 21, 1872, which he had circulated to every ratepayer in the town. In it he explains why he had resigned from the Corporation the previous year, vowing not to re-enter it until its character changed.

"I would not associate with some of its members," he told the town. "I entered the Corporation when it was an honour coveted by some of the best men in the town. I left it because it had, through some of its members, become a byword and a reproach. We want men of character, position, intelligence and honour." In this instance he was not referring only to Williams but to another Councillor whom he constantly accused of stealing, and ultimately hounded to death.

It was not until 1889 that the Fairfield Recreation Ground was properly laid out and formally declared open. John Williams was not there. He had died suddenly on June 26, 1872, his end hastened, it was said, by the effort expended on his cherished Fairfield and enmity aroused in those who thought that a piece of land without a building on it was a financial crime. They could produce figures to support his view.

At the opening of Kingston Station in 1863 it was emphasised in the speeches that land which had sold for only £100 an acre before the railway was now fetching £800 and more. Two years earlier, during a court action, it was stated that land on the Fairfield was fetching up to £1,200 an acre.

Williams, who had also played a prominent part in improving education facilities in Kingston, and in helping the poor, whose plight he understood so well from his own early experiences, received in death the adulation denied him in life. Crowds lined the streets as his funeral procession traversed the town, led by the band of the 3rd Royal Surrey Militia, and many thousands thronged Kingston Cemetery for his interment.

Ald Gould was conspicuous by his absence from the civic part of the procession. It was also noted that his was the only shop in the town not to have its shutters up as a sign of mourning!

He must have been chagrined by the inscription that was engraved on Williams' polished granite headstone. It records that John Williams "by his efforts and liberality succeeded in securing for the enjoyment of the public the recreation ground opened in the Fairfield and in improving the Promenade on the banks of the Thames . . ."

Gould can, however, rejoice in spirit that Williams' grave, together with its inscription, is today almost totally hidden by a holly tree, and that his name is unknown to those who now enjoy the green space he sacrificed so much to achieve.

Shortly before the Fairfield controversy, Queen's Promenade had opened with a flourish in August 1856, when Queen Victoria drove along the new road running beside it, accompanied by the Prince Consort and the Princess Royal.

"Hooray for the Queen's Parade," roared the thousand schoolchildren who lined the route. And that is how this stretch of road, previously called Town's End, became Queen's Parade, then Queen's Road. Now, prosaically, it is known simply as the start of Portsmouth Road. However, the riverside walk that runs parallel with it still retains the regal name of Queen's Promenade.

It was a magnificent improvement to the town. Until the 1850's, the river frontage in Portsmouth Road had been ugly and dangerous. A bed of fine gravel had been worked out until the foreshore was pitted with deep holes. These excavations had so weakened the foundations of the main road that sections of it frequently fell away and were shored up with bits of timber. This was a menance to pedestrians and vehicles alike because, though the river was some 15 feet deep along this stretch, it was protected only by a row of old white posts and a wooden rail.

A further hazard was a great bend in the river, from Surbiton Road to the Anglers' pub, (which stood at the junction of South Lane and is now replaced by a block of offices and flats). This bend forced the main road into a dangerously awkward angle that was the cause of many accidents.

Public meetings had been held in Kingston during the 1820's to discuss the problem and Brunel, one of the most famous engineers of the day, had been called in. His scheme for filling in the river bend cost an estimated £4,000. This was beyond Kingston's means, and the river road was left to crumble.

Two unusually resourceful men ended this dismal situation. One was William Woods, the developer responsible for many of the fine houses in and around the Portsmouth Road. The other was Frederick Gould, who had come to Kingston from Bath in 1839 and never let the town forget the fact until his death in 1900. He was tiresome company, as fond of his own voice as of heaping praise upon himself. Nevertheless, he got things done and we still enjoy the fruits of his labours today.

William Woods knew that the riverside improvement would add to the value of the 300 elegant houses he was building. In fact, he was already planning a raised riverside walk between Ravens Ait and St Raphael's Church for the exclusive use of people residing in his houses. This he could do because he held the land on a long lease from the Corporation. On meeting Gould, he undertook to pay for this promenade, and hand it and the lease to the people of the town, provided the remaining stretch from St Raphael's to the Anglers was accomplished at public expense.

The Corporation wanted no part in it, but Gould had an inspiration. As chairman of Kingston's Board of Surveyors, he had found that vast quantities of dirt were removed from the roads each year, and he arranged that it should be dumped on the river bank. At the same time, Chelsea Waterworks Co. had just begun massive excavations for reservoirs and filter beds along the Portsmouth Road. The company agreed to give all their excavated earth to the scheme, their contractors hauling it up to the bend, and so gradually filling it in, at an agreed price of 3d. a yard. Then Gould called on the City of London Corporation. They refused to give money, but they provided all the necessary work boats and tackle. They also gave the services of their engineer and surveyor, Mr S.W. Leath. He prepared the plans and supervised operations while Gould continued to amass thousands of tons of earth and dirt between 1852 and 1854.

At last there was sufficient. The river bend was filled in to provide a good, straight road. The old public landing, known as Rampier Wharf, was moved up to what we now know as Town End Wharf, and the raised river walk was completed.

It was a complex operation, begun before the Crimea War, continued throughout it, and completed at the time of the peace celebrations. Yet the whole scheme cost Kingston only £712 in private subscriptions, and it was remarked at the subscribers' meeting afterwards that Gould had been seen working on the site himself day after day, in all weathers.

This improvement attracted many more people to Kingston and gave a much-needed boost to trade. Yet, incredibly, the notorious local apathy was soon in evidence. Once built, the riverside promenade was so neglected that within five years of its Royal inauguration the river bank was crumbling away through lack of maintenance, and the once beautiful shrubbery was an overgrown mass.

"The promenade is an attraction possessed by very few towns . . . tradesmen are blind to their own interests to see it fall into decay year after year," declared the *Surrey Comet* of October 1864. "When we consider that Mr Woods expended £1,000 on a portion of it before he gave it up to the public, we feel some disappointment at the small sum obtained by public subscription.

Restoration work eventually went ahead, and the promenade was increased in width from 20 to 30 feet. But it was two years before sufficient funds dribbled in to complete the task. In fact, it probably never would have been completed but for John Williams, who fought long and hard, and dug deep into his own pocket, to preserve the promenade for posterity. In this, as with his Fairfield campaign, he was rewarded with loud hostility led by Frederick Gould. Gould was evidently a tireless worker for schemes initiated by himself. He was less dedicated if the limelight was diverted. It is interesting to note that the restored promenade was largely constructed of stone from the old Blackfriars Bridge, built in the 1760's and replaced by a new bridge 100 years later.

In 1896, thanks to Ald Joseph Marsh, Queen's Promenade was extended. He had hoped that swimming baths would be built under the extension, but the Council did not agree. He had to be content with a bandstand instead, where the Kingston and Surbiton Promenade Band gave concerts in the summer.

The new extension was ceremoniously opened on June 10, but the weather was so wet that scarcely anyone turned up.

* * * * * * * * *

Alderman Gould often claimed credit for Canbury Gardens. However, the real inspiration for this beautiful riverside garden was Samuel Gray, whose family had been prosperous maltsters and lightermen in Kingston since the 18th century.

Gray was a founder of the Canbury Ratepayers' Association, formed early in the 1880's to give this developing and somewhat despised part of the town a voice in public affiars. It succeeded. Many of its members were subsequently elected as councillors and had a profound effect on the council's social and political complexion.

Gray remembered the Canbury riverside in pre-railway days when, as recorded by George Ayliffe, it was "swamp land and osier beds, where snipe abounded and the beautiful kingfisher . . . the cottage by the towing path was occupied by Mr Stevens, a boatman, after whom Stevens Eyots are still named."

After the arrival of the railway and its attendant building expansion, the site became a tar factory and foul rubbish dump before, thanks to Samuel Gray, being transformed into the gardens that did so much to raise the residential attractions of Canbury.

On June 9, 1884 Mr Gray called a public meeting of Canbury residents in the old iron room of St Luke's Church. Here he revealed his riverside plans for the first time and moved a resolution "that the ground on the river bank known as the eyots be laid out as a public garden."

Later that year he was elected councillor for Canbury Ward and on May 26, 1887 introduced the Canbury Gardens proposition into the council chamber. He moved "that the Improvement, Property and Sanitary Committee be instructed to remove as soon as possible from the river bank, known as the Upper Eyot, the tar paving manufactory, the road materials and other miscellaneous and unsavoury objects deposited there . . . and that the view from the river shall be a pleasant one and not, as at present, unsightly and obnoxious."

The motion was defeated, after councillors objected that if such a garden was created "it would be used by working men."

Undeterred, Gray raised the matter again in October 1888, declaring that the improvement would not only "bring the town up to a level with other places, such as Richmond" but would help to fill the rapidly increasing number of unlet houses in the borough.

That argument won the day. The meeting agreed to Gray's resolution that plans should be draw up "for the whole of the land known as the Corporation Eyot."

The plans were prepared by the borough surveyor, Henry Macaulay, and in August, 1889, Mr Samuel Atkins of Queen Elizabeth Road was contracted to construct the first section, extending a thousand feet from the new Down Hall road "to a point in line with Kings Road." The work cost £404. 10s. and was completed in February 1890. Further extensions, plus turfing and landscaping, continued for the rest of the decade, and was largely supervised by the aged Ald Gould, who went there daily in his bathchair and found it an absorbing interest until his death in 1900.

Canbury Gardens proved to be one of the most popular amenities ever provided in the town and a triumph for Samuel Gray who, though wealthy enough to live in a far more fashionable locality, chose to build himself a house at 2 Gibbon Road, where he lived for many years, and where he died in 1914.

* * * * * * * * *

The 19th century had nearly run its course when Kingston finally achieved its own elegant theatre.

Its forerunner was the Albany Hall, built in Fife Road by Mr George Bristow in 1883. Mr Bristow as a dedicated disciple of the temperance movement and his new hall, opened in October, was mainly devoted to events of a religious or "improving" sort. According to a description in the *Kingston and Surbiton News* of October 13, 1883 it was a galleried building, seating 800, and illuminated by a handsome glass chandelier suspended from the centre ceiling.

Its existence was shortlived. In February, 1897 it became the property of the Kingston-on-Thames Theatre Company and was converted into the Royal County Theatre.

"No-one who can recall the many useful purposes to which the Albany Hall has been put can see its career ended without a feeling of regret," said the *Kingston and Surbiton News* of January 30, noting that the celebrated chandelier had fetched one shilling at auction.

The theatre, a showpiece which cost the then huge sum of £18,000 to construct, enjoyed 11 good years as a home for opera, drama and pantomime. Then, from 1908, cars and electric trams began drawing people to the more famous theatres of London. The advent of films was a further blow, and the theatre ran at a heavy loss. In November 1912 the company conceded defeat and the theatre became a cinema owned by Perfect Playhouses Ltd. Bankruptcy closed its doors in 1913, and it had two more unsuccessful owners before it was re-opened for the fourth time as the Super Cinema. Many people remember this place with nostalgia, even though they claim that rats and fleas were among the regular patrons!

What looked like a glittering new chapter began in 1939 when H. and R. Properties took over the building and spent a large sum on new furnishings and equipment. Soon afterwards, in February 1940, the building was gutted by fire. After lying derelict for years, it was acquired by Times Furnishing, who built a new store on the site.

However, a little of this once fine Victorian theatre remains. From Clarence Street, the word THEATRE is still faintly visible on Times Furnishing's south wall.

The Pioneers of New Malden

"There is something very irrepressible about our New Malden friends . . . opposition seems but to stimulate them to bolder action,," remarked the *Surrey Comet* of December 17, 1870.

It was true. For spirit and what can only be called sheer bloody-mindedness, the New Malden pioneers had few equals.

Until 1836, the area had been just a stretch of open country separated from Kingston by the great open acres of Norbiton Common. Then the London and Southampton Railway was constructed across the Common en route to Surbiton, to be followed in 1846 by the station of New Malden with Coombe, opened on September 1. The line from Kingston was cut through the fields of Dickerage Farm, and opened in 1869.

New Malden's beginnings were remarkably similar to those of Surbiton. Both had always been isolated country areas, consisting mainly of common; both had railways carved through their quiet green spaces in the middle 1830's; both were to fight – and win – wars of independence against Kingston; and both owed their birth to the perspicacity of a single individual in each case. In Surbiton that individual was a Kingston maltster named Thomas Pooley. In New Malden it was a Kingston draper named John King. There the similarities ended. Surbiton was planned from the outset as a place of charm and opulence. New Malden, on the other hand, was for years an ill-favoured huddle at the foot of elegant Coombe Hill. Its 19th century history of continuous, and often hilarious, cussedness would make marvellous television viewing today.

John King's drapery emporium was at 1 Thames Street. It is now the home of the Bradford and Bingley Building Society, but its former owner has been immortalised in the name of King's Passage, the medieval alley to the riverside which bounds the south side of the premises.

Mr King was one of Kingston's leading personalities. He and Thomas Fricker were the last to hold the office of Bailiff, an ancient appointment that was superseded by the mayoral system from 1836.

Later, in 1840, Mr King served as Mayor and also became an alderman and borough magistrate. He was a champion huntsman, who rode regularly with the Royal and Surrey Staghounds. William Drewett has recalled the colourful sight of King and neighbouring tradesmen from the Market Place riding off to the meet in their scarlet coats.

John King, like Thomas Pooley, was one of the first Kingstonians to realise that the railways would bring social and economic revolution. In 1835, three years before the first local station opened at Surbiton, he bought 93 acres of farm and common land. It stretched north and south between what is now Kingston Road and the foot of Coombe Hill, and east and west between what is now Coombe Road and Elm Road. Frederick Merryweather has recorded Mr King paid £3,900 for his purchase, but he got it back many times over. He sold some of the land to the London and South Western Railway Company, and to Lambeth Waterworks. But his major coup came in 1850, when he sold 57 acres north of the railway line to the National Freehold Land Society for £4,562.

His acres south of the line went to a Mr Gover for what chronicler Frederick Merryweather called "a goodly sum." With these transactions, Mr King could be said to have founded New Malden.

The first part of the new town to appear was the six groves – Acacia, Chestnut, Lime, Sycamore, Poplar and Elm – laid out by the National Freehold Land Society during the 1850's and planted with trees to match their names. The first residents arriving at what they thought would be a fresh and leafy village, had a rude awakening. The roads were appalling. There was no drainage, no mains water, no lighting and a stinking open sewer ran down what is now the High Street.

Mr Kent, Kingston's medical officer reported in June 1866 that all the drainage in New Malden was defective.

"In Malden Grove, commonly called The Barracks, large pools of dirty water impregnated with sewage stand in back gardens," he said. He added that the whole of the New Malden sewage was carried along Coombe Road in an open ditch, the smell from which was "almost intolerable", which emptied into a small stream at the bottom of Coombe Hill.

(The reference to "The Barracks" is interesting. It supports a tradition that dwellings in what is now called Cleveland Road were once used by the militia, officers and their families being quartered in the villas and troops in the cottages.)

However, there was the railway station. The service to London would, it was believed, soon attract more residents and New Malden would improve.

The pioneer settlers soon realised that the rest of the world regarded their village as a primitive nonentity. The lead was set by the gentry of Coombe, who were so appalled at the prospect of a new town developing close to their country retreats that they brought influence to bear on the railway company. At first only three trains a day were allowed to stop at New Malden en route to the then terminus at Vauxhall. By 1857 there were seven trains a day to Waterloo, but the *Surrey Comet* of July 4 was complaining that the station was "in a dangerous condition and resembles a cattle station." At a public meeting on March 19, 1883 the station was described as "a collection of wooden shanties." The meeting, reported in the *Kingston and Surbiton News* of March 24, also heard how two developers who had intended to build elegant villas in New Malden arrived at the station, took one disgusted look at the platform, and travelled straight back to London. By then a hundred trains were stopping at the station every 24 hours, but the developers were not impressed, declaring that "one could never induce a lady or gentleman to go down a gully like this." Queen Victoria refused to set foot on the platform. When she arrived for visits to the stately homes of Coombe, she alighted at Norbiton Station instead. It was a wise decision in view of some of the extra-mural activities at New Malden station. On one occasion, for instance, a clergyman named Cotton laid a wager with one of the local cabbies that he could race him up the stone steps to the railway platform on horseback. The reverend gentleman won.

The Lambeth Water Co. was as cavalier as the railway company. They deigned to connect New Malden to their mains and collect a substantial rate, but they did not provide a regular turncock to turn on the supply each day.

By the end of the 1850's there were some 900 people living amid the mire and muck of New Malden. According to Frederick Merryweather, Kingston Corporation, to whom they paid rates, refused to provide street lighting or adequate rubbish removal. The MP for West Surrey, Mr Henry Drummond, was equally contemptuous. The villagers approached him in 1856 for a subscription towards their first church in Poplar Grove. His reply was brutal: "There is no more need for a church than there is of a town."

New Maldenites decided the time had come for some of the famous bloody-mindedness that enlivened local newspapers until the end of the century. They snapped their fingers at Kingston and their MP and on December 3, 1866 established their own New Malden Local Board. It soon showed its mettle. The Lambeth Water Co., prompted by the implacable toughness of the Board, supplied a regular turncock. Roads and drainage were improved. Then it was time to deal with Richmond, which was urgently in need of a sewage scheme. It did not wish to pollute its own elegant atmosphere, so decided to send all its effluent to New Malden instead, earmarking 224 acres of Blagdon Farm for the purpose. The Board rose in wrath. An inquiry was ordered in 1871, Richmond's scheme was rejectd and the Board earned the famous title of "plucky little Malden."

It was equally determined in dealing with the gas works. In 1857 Messrs A. Jonson, H. Weber, J. Ponder and McGill had launched the New Malden Gas, Coal and Coke Co. in what had first been known as Thompson's Lane, then as Elm Grove and is today Elm Road. Their advertisement in the *Surrey Comet* of June 27 promised "a new process, giving gas of a superior quality." Nevertheless, the stench from the works was so appalling it made people ill.

In 1868, the New Malden Board went to law against the then owner of the gas works, a Mr Ebenezer Viney. There was a courtroom battle that made lively reading in the *Surey Comet* of February 27. The gas holder was described as "an old, rusty article," so unsafe that in windy weather it had to be held down by force, and so full of holes that "it was no uncommon thing to see the manager on a fine morning lying down on the top of it, stopping up the cracks with white lead."

The manager, Mr Bliss, declared on oath that the smell from the works was good for people because it made them sick, and so cleansed their systems. He described how he had cured five of his children of whooping cough by putting them in the boiler. Cross-examined, he admitted that they had developed scarlet fever immediately afterwards but, he said, "I popped them in the purifier again and the fever disappeared." In any case, added Mr Bliss, New Malden deserved all it got because the people would not pay their bills.

"I often have to call three times for an account of tenpence for a quarter's supply," he said.

Neither he nor Mr Viney could beat New Malden Board. Mr Viney was fined £2 for causing a nuisance. By July Kingston Gas Co. had taken over his works, pulled down the offending factory and connected their mains at Kingston with the service pipes at new Malden. That year the village streets were lit by public gas lamps for the first time.

However, nothing could compare with the row when it was decided to build a new school.

In 1855 the villagers had built the temporary church of St James in Poplar Grove as their first place of worship. By 1866 they were able to build the present Christ Church on a site in Coombe Road given by the Duke of Cambridge, and St James was converted into a day and Sunday school which provided the first education available in New Malden.

Soon there was need both for a larger school and for a village institute, and it was decided to erect a building that could serve both purposes. A building committee, led by churchwarden Mr Frederick Merryweather, raised the money and the building of Christ Church School in Lime Grove was completed in 1870. Then the Vicar, the Revd Charles Stirling, suddenly decreed it would be the work of the devil to allow non-educational activities to take place in a Church of England school. He banned Mr Merryweather from worship, declaring that "Satan had hold of him." He then set up a Vicar's Defence Committee to give him sole rights over the school. The Defence Committee also produced its own weekly publication – "and a more vile, scurrilous and libellous document was never penned, disgraceful alike to the author and the printing office where it was issued," declared the *Surrey Comet* in July 1870.

In October the Charity Commissioners decreed that the school could be used for educational purposes only, whereupon the Vicar and his supporters decided to ban the building committee from its doors.

> "The excitement in the village was brought to a grand climax when the Vicar and other persons, among whom was a man said to have been brought from London for the purpose, wended their way to the new school to take forcible possession," reported the *Surrey Comet* in November. "Inside the building were three members of the Building Committee, and by picking up forms and desks a stand was made for a time against the attacks of the invaders. At last the door was smashed in and the Vicar and his friends made good their entry – how far a dignified entry the reverend gentleman is best able to judge."

Things did not end there. As the election of the school managers drew near, the Vicar made frantic efforts to ensure that only his nominees were appointed.

> "Votes were eagerly paid for, and so fearful was the Vicar of defeat that upwards of £90 was paid in by Mr Stirling and his friends for votes purchased that day," said the *Surrey Comet*.

The Vicar triumphed and was set to rule supreme over church and school. However, he reckoned without the determination of Mr Merryweather and his band. They had proved they did not need Kingston or their MP. Now they proved they did not need their parish church either. On December 20, 1870 they opened their own breakaway church on a site in Malden Road. The new place of worship, an iron structure seating 300 and dedicated to the Holy Trinity, was described as "free Church of England".

The *Surrey Comet* of December 17 said it had been opened "by members of the Church of England who are prevented from attending the place of worship they assited to erect and maintain. That its erection should be found necessary must surely be deplored by all churchmen, and there can be but one conclusion drawn therefrom."

To make the Vicar's discomfiture complete, the rebels also provided a large iron room to be used for Sunday School on the Sabbath and for meetings and social events during the week. It was officially named the New Malden Institute and opened in January 1871 with a celebration tea at which every seat was taken and extra tables had to be brought in. Thereafter it became the local government HQ and the general pivot of village activities.

Mr Stirling's views on Satan evidently underwent rapid change. During the first three months of 1871 the *Surrey Comet* carried detailed reports of readings, concerts and other entertainments being held on the same nights at the same time at Lime Grove School, with the Vicar in the chair, and at the New Malden Institute, with Mr Merryweather presiding. These reports were always placed adjacent so readers could chart the progress of the two sides in their fierce competition for audiences. On balance, Mr Stirling seems to have attracted the wealthy residents of Coombe while Mr Merryweather basked in the less erudite patronage of the village.

By March, 1871 the Institute had set up a public library. It opened with 300 donated books that even Mr Stirling could not fault.

"The volumes have been selected with great care, chiefly from the catalogues of the Pure Literature Society, the Religious Tract Society and the Sunday School Union," reported the *Surrey Comet.*

A piquant element in the Stirling/Merryweather war was that Mr Merryweather was still officially Vicar's Warden. As such he attended the Easter Vestry of 1871 which, in the words of the *Surrey Comet,* "brought scenes hitherto unparalleled in this district."

The war went on for years. By 1883 the Holy Trinity rebels were able to replace their temporary church with a handsome stone one, designed by Mr Lockwood Heward, surveyor to New Malden Board. At its opening on December 17 the minister, the Revd Professor Bradshaw, made reference to "every church in New Malden being on the point of a dagger with every other church."

The dramatic departure of Mr Stirling after 27 years as Vicar heralded the end of this extraordinary saga. He left in November 1892 amid a blaze of national publicity after announcing his seccession from the Church of England.

> "I respond to the call of duty and quit the pale of the Romanised and Romanising establishment in the hope of being a pioneer in the work of forming a Protestant church of England (with a prayerbook purged of every vestige of sacerdotalism and sacramental error) which may rally to itself all that is good and holy in the land and prove a beacon light in these dark and dangerous days to England, to her colonies and to the world," he announced in a public statement addressed to "Protestants of the British Empire."

His decision prompted a wave of controversy throughout the land. It also sent a wave of relief through the breweries of Kingston.

For Mr Stirling was an implacable enemy of alcohol and it was largely thanks to him that the Temperance Gospel Mission could claim, as they did prior to the licensing sessions in March 1883, that of New Malden's population of 2,500, no fewer than 600 were teetotallers.

They turned their full force on Fricker's Eagle Brewery of Kingston, who were seeking to build a pub on the embryonic Mount Pleasant estate.

The abstainers declared that if young men would save a few pence each day, instead of drinking it, they would have a large sum by the time they were 35. Fricker's retorted that over-eating was as harmful as overdrinking, and recommended the teetotallers to save threepence a day in eating so that by the time they were 35 they could buy a coffin and decently inter themselves! The magistrates were not amused. Fricker's application was rejected, as were many similar ones in the village.

Charles Stirling has had a lasting influence on his former parish. One of his first acts as Vicar was to form a Trust to ensure that only men of "Protestant evangelical" principles should succeed him. This has been adhered to at Christ Church, as has Mr Stirling's teetotal principles. To this day no intoxicants are served, not even at weddings or social events in the church halls.

Mr Stirling's departure, and his replacement by the Revd William Challacombe, left the way clear for Frederick Merryweather and his friends to return to the Christ Church fold.

Holy Trinity closed and was eventually bought by Mr Graham Spicer for use as a Boys' Bible class and institute. The building still survives in New Malden High Street.

* * * * * * * * *

Simultaneous with hostilities in church, war was being waged within New Malden's Local Board. The issue, which split the membership into two camps and led to the resignation of Mr Merryweather, was Benjamin Looker's plan for a new pottery works on 14 acres of the Blagdon Farm fields in what is now Blagdon Road.

Looker's Pottery and Brickworks had been founded some half-century earlier by Mr Looker's father, Benjamin senior, who ran a building yard in Kingston's Clarence Street before acquiring some acres on what were then the lonely slopes of Kingston Hill. It was heavy clay land, and here Mr Looker established brickfields on a site extending from what is now the Albert Hotel up to what is now Crescent Road. At a meeting of the Assessment Committee in December 1861 the site was said to produce about 900,000 bricks a year and to be equipped with a 10 h.p. engine and a pattern room.

When the clay on the Kingston Hill site had been exhausted the firm, which had been inherited by Benjamin Looker junior and his twin brothers, moved to Norbiton Common. Old field names, such as Clay Close, Tilehouse Close and the close "where the tile kiln lately stood" indicate that this had long been prime pottery territory. Ordnance Survey maps show that at various times in the Victorian era there were brickfields on both sides of Kingston Road. One, on the north side, extended from what is now Waters Road to Dickerage Lane, bounded on the north by the Kingston branch railway.

Another, on the south side of Kingston Road, occupied part of what later became Malden and Coombe Sewage Works, and is remembered today in the name of Potters Grove. There was a third at what is now the Fountain Roundabout.

Benjamin Looker junior, was an early member of New Malden Local Board and eventually decided to set up his own pottery in the village, independent of his brothers. There was uproar when he submitted his drawings to the planning committee in January, 1877. By March, infuriated by the wrangling, he proceeded to construct his works without approval. By April, Merryweather had resigned from the Board in protest. By the end of the year New Malden Pottery and Brickwsorks was a reality.

After Benjamin Looker's death in 1892, the new pottery owners outraged local residents by introducing traction engines. These ran to and from the brickworks drawing heavy waggons and were said "frequently to exceed the speed limit of 4 m.p.h."

A letter in the *Kingston and Surbiton News* of July 15, 1899 described the suffering inflicted by the machines.

"At six in the morning the inhabitants are shaken in their beds, and just as they recover from the first shock, the earth trembles once more; and so on throughout several days of the week. Ceilings have fallen down, ornaments have been shaken off mantelpieces and even birds' eggs have been shaken out of their nests by this terrible nuisance."

The statement from New Malden Ratepayers' Association was stronger. It complained of "the frequent perambulations of the district by two rattling, noisy, dangerous, stinking machines of the Pottery Company, red hot cinders spraying out of their funnels".

Eventually it was decided to hold a Local Government Board Inquiry into the nuisance, but it disappeared before the Inquiry could take place. In Kingston County Court on January 12, 1900 Judge Sidney Lushington ordered that New Malden Potteries should be wound up after hearing that the firm had £10,000 in capital and no assets to meet liabilities. On February 15, Messrs Hawes auctioned off all the machinery and plant by Sheriff's order. Advertisements for the sale indicate the scope of the firm which, for all its unpopularity, was an important source of local employment. Sale items included:

"A 35 h.p. compound engine and boiler by Davey Paxman and Co. of Colchester; an electric light engine and dynamo by Johnson of Leeds; a steam wire brick-cutter by Bennet and Sayer of Derby; a 10 h.p. portable engine and boiler by Taxford and Son; steam pug mill, grinding mill, large Cornish boiler and two hand brick presses; 200,000 good hard burnt red bricks; 10,000 unburnt bricks; 30,000 flower pots; 50 tons of coal; a copying press and "a useful grey cob." *The Kingston and Surbiton News* reported that buyers from all over the country paid high prices.

"But nothing was seen of the objectionable traction engines, which we understand were held on the hire purchase system and were removed some weeks ago," it added.

Shortly after the sale, the newspapers reported that the erstwhile secretry of the Potteries, Mr Atterbury, had swallowed his false teeth and been rushed to hospital.

Potteries remained in Blagdon Road for many more years. The clay was exhausted by the 1920's. Then the pits were replenished with a free supply excavated during extensions to the Underground railway from Clapham to Morden. By 1938 the clay was again exhausted, and only flowerpots could be made. However, during World War II the firm secured a contract with the Ministry of Food to dry out water-damaged cereals in the brick-drying plant. Early in the war, the empty claypits were bought by Malden and Coombe Council, who used them as a public tip. After the war, there was a local schools' half-holiday when the giant chimney, built by Benjamin Looker some 65 years previously, was demolished. However, Looker's Kingston Hill pits survive as ornamental lakes in the grounds of the Lakeside flats.

Merryweather's break with New Malden's Local Board soon healed. When the Board was promoted to the status of an Urban District Council, he was elected chairman at the first meeting on New Year's Day, 1895. He died in 1900 having, like his old adversary Charles Stirling, formed a lasting influence on New Malden.

New Malden's Trade and Development

Despite the tough individualism of its leaders, and their frequent jibes against unprogressive Kingston, New Malden's development was slow and its trade moribund for most of the 19th century. A major disappointment was that the population increased by fewer than a hundred each year. In 1865 there were approximately 1,200 residents. In 1871 there were 1,606. In 1883 there were still only 2,500.

Land speculators had an anxious time. The development of Mount Pleasant, for example, began in 1880. Three years later only four houses had been built, of which only one was occupied. Thirty years on, as shown by the Ordance Survey, the situation had scarcely changed. It was much the same with the Norbiton Park area. Roads were laid out in the 80's and 90's, but there were few houses in them until well into the 20th century. Those that were built were seldom high-class structures. At worst they were inferior cottages. At best they were what Dr Beale Collins' local medical report in 1894 called "one servant villas, a degree higher up the social scale than Kingston."

This had a depressing effect on rates revenue and on local business. In 1870, for instance, the landlord of the Norbiton Park Hotel went bankrupt because of what was described in court as "stagnation of trade in the neighbourhood." This hotel, incidentally, was later re-named the Fountain in honour of the drinking fountain "for man and beast" set up at the junction of Kingston, Malden and Burlington Roads by the local branch of the Band of Mercy in 1894. The original fountain was demolished by a vehicle in 1932. Fifty years later the Rotary Club of New Malden provided a replacement. This structure, 30-feet high and made of metal, timber and fibreglass, now graces The Fountain Roundabout, constructed at the junction in 1982 at a cost of £23,000.

Other causes for New Malden's dismal trading are evident in the *Surrey Comet's* comments of January 25, 1897 on learning that a co-operative store might be opened in the stretch of Coombe Road that the Local Board in 1868 had optimistically re-named Market Place. At the same time they had re-named the road running across Norbiton Common Kingston Road instead of Cambridge Road.

> "It is alleged that the quality of the articles sold by the tradesmen of New Malden is inferior and the prices high," declared the *Surrey Comet.* "We should be sorry to see this project carried out, for many of the tradespeople there find business bad enough as it is. Perhaps, however, they may take a wholesome hint from the circular and render the cooperative project abortive by selling goods of the best quality at a moderate price and by conducting their business with promptitude and civility."

The only inducement to live in the village would seem to have been good health. Mr Child, the medical officer, reported in February 1881 that, while Kingston had a death rate of 17.3 per thousand and Surbiton 14.3, the death rate in New Malden was only 9.5.

"Health figures show there is no village which exceeds for salubrity the village of New Malden, where the death rate for several years has been less than 1%," commented the *Surrey Comet's* leader column. It added that, though there was much cottage property and a primitive drainage system in New Malden, the air there was "remarkably pure" because it was protected from the north by Coombe Hill and open to breezes from the south.

Law and order left much to be desired. In May 1879 the Comet was demanding: "Where are the Police at New Malden?" and reporting that hooliganism was being ignored because the constables were "indifferent or afraid."

However, the real reason for unchecked crime was lack of a police station. Eventually, after decades of delay, news came in 1890 that the village was about to have its own station at the junction of the Burlington and Malden Roads.

> "Although possibly an undesirable institution to the inhabit ants, the station will be a great boon to the police of the district, for at present constables are compelled to walk with the lawbreakers they may happen to apprehend to Kingston, Epsom or Wimbledon," declared the *Kingston and Surbiton News* of July 5, 1890. "The effect of this, according to rumour, is that cases are often passed over."

The building opened in March 1892, complete with a covered parade ground, cells and a measuring rack for prisoners. Evidently the authorities had decided to make up for lost time. "It is no exaggeration to say that the building is bigger than the police station to be found in many towns ten times as populous as this district," remarked the *Kingston and Surbiton News.*

In 1886 the Local Board managed to scrape together an annual grant of £20 towards the establishment on April 27 of the "Number 6 Fire Station", organised at New Malden by the Kingston and Surbiton Voluntary Fire Brigade.

> "The appliances consist of a light car, six lengths of hose, standpipe and hand pump, brought over and lodged on Mr Montague's premises," revealed the *Kingston and Surbiton News* on May 1.

Thomas Montague, a baker in Market Place, was appointed chief-in-command of the new station, with Messrs Thomas, Giblett and Andrews as volunteer firemen.

It was a dangerously inadequate arrangement. The equipment was of the most primitive kind, kept in a private shed which, as the *Kingston and Surbiton News* so rightly said, was "out of sight and probably unknown as to existence to most persons in the neighbourhood."

Largely due to Mr Montague's perseverance, the Duke of Cambridge presented a site in Market Place for the construction of a proper fire station. The Local Board would not, or could not find the £200 needed for the work. The local residents would not, or could not, support Mr Montague's appeal for voluntary subscriptions. Not until 1905 did a purpose-built fire station materialise. In the meantime the Brigade had to make do with any hut or barn it could find – first in Market Place, then in Acacia Grove, and finally in Cambridge Road.

They gained some consolation by managing to raise £50 for a one-horse curricle in 1891. This boasted a two-handled pump which required six men, but could shoot a jet of water 50 feet. Only in May 1904 did the village acquire its first steam fire engine, a Shand Mason model.

Conditions were no more luxurious for New Malden's rulers. From 1871, when they had mere Local Board status, and for the first decade of their career from 1895 as the Maldens and Coombe District Council, they had met on hired premises described in Press reports as so cold that members often had to swathe themselves in rugs, and so fetid that they sometimes had to rush outside to be sick.

For nearly 40 years there were arguments over whether New Malden should have proper municipal premises. The question was resolved on April 27, 1905 with the opening by Viscount Middleton of new council offices in Coombe Road, with a fire station adjoining. Flags flew, bands played and among the guests was the indomitable clergyman Charles Stirling, then aged 79, who had been elected first chairman of New Malden Board nearly 40 years previously. The new buildings were designed by architect Mr W. H. Hope of Hampton Wick and built by Messrs Goddard of Farnham at a cost of £6,000.

The root cause of stagnation in New Malden was the appalling state of the station. The village had been planned around the railway. Speculators were confident that prosperous commuters would be eager to settle in such a healthy spot, served by both a main and a branch railway. The physical condition of the station toppled these hopes. Finally, in March 1883, residents organised a public meeting to adopt a memorial to the London and South Western Railway demanding "a new station with a suitable carriage drive." A variety of evidence, including the depressing population figures already quoted, was given to show how the station was keeping people away. It was recalled that the station had started as "nothing but a box with a ladder leading up to it." Thirty-six years later things had improved slightly, but the ascent to the platforms was still so arduous that one ratepayer suggested it be re-named the New Malden Gymnasium! A deputation was picked to wait on the railway company asking for the station to be re-sited so the hated steps could be done away with. The railway company, with its total monopoly, refused. Until the end of the century passengers to New Malden frequently had to travel in the luggage van, and conditions at the station were bad enough for the Ratepayers' Association to describe the railway company as "a nest of brigands." Nevertheless, some improvements were made and, slight as they were, they did help the village.

The scope of New Malden's Local Authority, and the rateable value at its disposal, was considerably enhanced in 1895, when it was made a District Council, and Malden and Coombe added to its territory. In 1891, New Malden Local Board presided over a population of 3,565. By 1905, when the new council offices were opened, Malden and Coombe District Council administered an area three times the size of Kingston, with a population of nearly 8,000.

But it was road, rather than rail, facilities that led to the true emergence of New Malden. In October 1927 the Prime Minister, Mr Stanley Baldwin, opened the Kingston By-pass as the first road of its kind in Britain. The following year the population of the Maldens and Coombe district was 20,180. By 1930 it had risen to 23,750 and the following year to 25,000.

Thus the area was thriving as never before when, like Surbiton, it was granted borough status in 1936. Residents mourned the loss of country atmosphere. No longer was it possible to walk to Surbiton across green fields. Nevertheless they continued, as many still do today, to refer always to New Malden as "the village."

In 1865 Malden and Coombe, together with Surbiton, were amalgamated with Kingston to form the Royal Borough of Kingston upon Thames. By then Malden and Coombe had nearly 47,000 residents, but the individualism planted by their 19th century forebears was unquenched. The merge with Kingston was reviled by the District Council as "grafting a healthy limb onto a decaying body!"

Down on the Farm in Malden

Throughout the 19th century, New Malden was surrounded by farms. On the Kingston side of Norbiton Common, to the east of what is now Hampden Road, was Wanderings Farm. The farmhouse, said to be more than 200 years old, survived until January 1959. Then it was demolished to make way for an extention to the Ralph Dark Tyre Works. Some of its original pastures remain as a recreation ground adjacent to Hampden Road.

Hoppingwood Farm had stood in peaceful isolation since the early 18th century. Then navvies arrived in the mid-1830's to bisect its lands with a railway line. Thereafter the infant New Malden grew up virtually at its gates. For the second half of the 19th century, and the first years of the 20th, the farm was occupied by the Horlick family. Their harvest homes, vividly described in contemporary issues of the *Surrey Comet,* were landmarks in the local calendar with their giant hams and cheeses and pitchers of cider, all consumed on upturned straw bales in the flickering light of lanters to the music of the local band, affectionately known as "the baby wakers." The farmhouse stood on a site today bounded by the Hoppingwood, Orchard, Alric and Cambridge Avenues. Many of its former 255 acres are now Malden Golf Course, Beverley Park and the Malden Wanderers' Cricket Club.

To the east, was Blagdon Farm and toward Motspur Park were Pritchett's Farm and Bluehouse Farm.

Travelling along Kingston Road, from what is now the Fountain Roundabout to Gloucester Road, all was arable and pasture land with scarcely a building in sight. Dickerage Lane was empty, save for Dickerage Farm at its northen end. On the south side of Kingston Road, the sole buildings were those of Norbiton Common Farm and Norbiton Park Farm.

On the Ordnance Survey map of 1866-68, both farms stand secluded amid their fields with no buildings anywhere in the vicinity. Between them lies Sow Lane, meandering its lonely way across the Hogsmill meadows towards Malden. On the Ordnance Survey of 1898-99, Norbiton Common Farm has a sewage works alongside, while Norbiton Park Farm is a tiny island surrounded by houses. On the 1914 map, Norbiton Park Farm has disappeared altogether. Sow Lane has been deodorised into South Lane, though it is still an undeveloped track. Norbiton Common Farm has become the Kingston Union Farm, where inmates from Kingston Workhouse were employed. Today Springfield Hospital stands on the site and the flat, windswept pastures have given way to Thorne, California, Beresford and Dunbar Roads.

Norbiton Park Farm made international headlines in the summer of 1862 when the dashing young former MP for Lambeth, William Roupell, confessed to frauds involving hundreds of thousands of pounds. Through forgery and deception, he had gained cash and property intended for his brothers and sisters in his father's will, and dissipated it all. Special prominence was given to the farm at Norbiton. This had been owned by Richard Palmer Roupell, founder of the family fortunes. After his death in 1856 a wealthy London tradesman named John Waite bought the farm from William Roupell, who claimed to own it by deed of gift from his father. In fact, the rightful owner was William's brother, Richard, who took legal action to eject Mr Waite from the property. The case was heard at Guildford Assizes and reported throughout Britain. It transpired that Roupell had raised £300,000 by fraud and spent it. He had pocketed £10,000 from the sale of Norbiton Park Farm.

"Roupell lived like a territorial grandee, sought by society into which money was a passport," commented *The Spectator* in August 1862. "He played high and lost always, contested Lambeth successfully and at excessive cost, and in five years fled, a hopelessly ruined man."

In September he was sentenced to penal servitude for life. Meanwhile Mr Waite retained possession of the farm and signalled his triumph by re-naming it Waitelands. By December of the following year Mr Waite was dead. Had he lived, Kingston might look very different today. For, as reiterated in a letter to the *Surrey Comet* of February 10, 1866, he had bought his farm with the intention of taking a railway through it, to terminate on the south side of the Fairfield in Kingston. This line, linking the City to Kingston, would have run across the Fairfield on an embankment 18 foot high. When the scheme was scotched, Mr Waite put all his strength behind the Kingston, Tooting and London Railway. This was to have two level crossings, one at Mitcham, the other on the road from Coombe to Malden, alongside his farmland. Even the fares had been set at 2d. per mile for first-class passengers, 1½d. for second and a penny for third. Mr Waite's death, just before the scheme was due to go before Parliament, was a bitter blow and the Kingston, Tooting and London Railway Bill was ultimately rejected.

By the 1880's the farm had been acquired by the London and Suburban Land Company and the Westbury, Sandal, Rodney and Presburgh Roads laid out. The farmhouse, situated on the south side of Park Road, survived into the 20th century. Now it and its lands are covered by the houses of Thetford, Nelson, Linton, Selwyn, Westbury, Park, Sandal, Rodney and Presburgh Roads, together with Albemarle Gardens and Elton Avenue.

North of New Malden, on either side of Coombe Lane West, were Coombelane Farm and Coombe Hill Farm.

The former was on the north side of the lane, and Kingston Hospital now stands on part of its former fields. For, in 1837, Thomas Dickins changed the landscape by selling five acres of his farmland to the Kingston Union for the great workhouse that was later to evolve into the many times greater Kingston Hospital.

Dickins sold the rest of the farm to the Duke of Cambridge in 1839. It survived until 1932, when the Duke's grandson, Sir Adolphus Fitz George, disposed of its 50 remaining acres for building. Today the farm is covered by Wolsey Close and flats and houses in Galsworthy Road.

Coombe Hill Farm was a far bigger enterprise. The Duke of Cambridge bought it from Earl Spencer in 1839 and, by enclosing land from Coombe Warren, increased it from 310 to 535 acres. However, this acreage decreased as sites were leased out for the building of Coombe's fine mansions. By 1897, there were 339 acres. By the early 1930's all but the house and a small island of land had been sold to developers for housing estates off Coombe Lane West. The farmhouse, an interesting 17th century building, was demolished in 1969 and replaced by Coombe Hill Junior and Infants' School.

The northern end of the Kingston By-Pass, with its attendant tides of traffic, was once part of Robin Hood Farm. This was established at least as early as 1737 – probably far earlier – with lush pastures stretching peacefully beside Beverley Brook. By the 1830's, when it was bought by the ubiquitous Duke of Cambridge, the farm had 129 acres of arable land and 59 acres of pasture. Its obliteration began early in the 1930's, when its acres were bisected north to south by the new Kingston By-pass, followed by the Kingston Vale housing estate.

The site of the farmhouse is now bounded by Bowness Crescent, Keswick Avenue, Robin Hood Way and part of Robin Hood Lane.

The Stately Homes of Coombe

While the stately homes of Kingston were being swept away by Victorian progress, a new generation of mansions was rising on Coombe Hill. This was the high-class section of the Maldens and Coombe administrative territory, clearly divided from the lower orders on the plains below.

Much of this aristocratic development remains intact today, giving the Royal Borough a uniquely beautiful period estate, rich in interest to students of Royal, topographical, social and literary history. Curiously, it is usually overlooked in accounts detailing places of local interest.

Coombe Manor and estate, in the parish of Kingston, had been owned by the 1st and 2nd Earls Spencer, ancestors of our Princess of Wales. In 1837, the 3rd Earl sold the estate for the 1st Duke of Cambridge, a son of George III. It comprised some 1,300 acres of woodland, heath, pasture and arable land and had been owned by the Spencers since 1753.

George, 2nd Duke of Cambridge and Commander-in-Chief of the British Army, inherited the estate from his father in 1850 and began leasing it out for building.

Its beauty, its proximity to London and the fact that there was a railway station nearby at New Malden made it an enticing prospect for wealthy families seeking a country seat. One of the first to recognise the possibilities was John Galsworthy, father of the famous author, who acquired 93 acres fronting what is now George Road on which to build three elegant mansions. While the building of the first was in progress, the Galsworthys lived at Parkfield on Kingston Hill, and it was here the author was born in 1867 (Parkfield is now a specialist centre for the treatment of alcoholism, and has been re-named Galsworthy House).

George Road then was just a cart track, with gravel pits occupying what is now the upper section of Coombe Wood Golf Course.

John Galsworthy has left us a vivid picture of how today's George Road and Warren Road looked until the late 19th century. It appears in

A Man of Property, in which he describes how Soames and Bosinney walked from Robin Hill Station to view a site for Soames' new house. Galsworthy later told the *Surrey Comet,* in a letter now preserved in the Borough Archives, that the station was the one at New Malden and the walk was along what are now the Warren and George Roads to his father's site. Here is an extract:

"They had struck into a half-made road across a warren. A cart track led at right angles to a gravel pit, beyond which the chimneys of a cottage rose amongst a clump of trees and the border of a thick wood.

"Tussocks of feathery grass covered the rough surface of the ground, and out of these the larks soared into a haze of sunshine. On the far horizon, over a countless succession of fields and hedges, rose a line of downs . . . the warren was as lonely as a prairie, its silence only broken by the rustle of rabbits bolting to their holes and the song of the larks. Soames felt his spirit daunted by the loneliness, by the invisible singing and the hot sweet air . . . almost from their feet stretched ripe corn, dipping to a small, dark copse beyond. A plain of fields and hedges spread to the distant blue-grey downs. In a silver streak to the right could be seen the line of the river. The sky was so blue, and the sun so bright, that an eternal summer seemed to reign over this prospect. Thistle-down floated round them, enraptured by the serenity of the ether. The heat danced over the corn, and brought a puff of warm air into their faces.

"'I could build you a teaser here,' said Bosinney. 'For about eight thousand I could build you a palace.'"

Certainly the first house built by Galsworthy senior was a 'teaser'. Known initially as Coombe Warren, and later as Coombe Court, it was to become world-famous as a centre of taste and opulent high living. To the Galsworthys, though, it was just a comfortable family home. The future author lived here for the first eight years of his life, and used it as one of the principal settings for his *Forsyte Saga.* In 1875 the estate was bought by Mr Daniel Watney of the famous brewing family, who landscaped the magnificent gardens stretching down to Coombe Lane West. Much of that landscaping still survives, including the rhododendrons and the ornamental lake, which now form part of The Drive.

When Mr Watney sold the estate in 1885, the advertisements not only provided a good description of the house, but indicated how Coombe had become established as a centre for the aristocracy:

". . . in close proximity to the seats of the Earl of Tankerville,

Lord Wolverton and Earl Dunraven, comprising 22 acres with 17 bedrooms, five bathrooms, boudoir, six lofty and well proportioned reception rooms (including double drawing room, music room and noble billiard room) schoolroom, entrance hall, vestibule and spacious lavatory. Also ample and complete domestic quarters, extensive cellarage heated with hot water, first class stabling for eight horses, coachman's cottage and grooms' rooms. Two lodge entrances, extensive range of glasshouses and forcing pits, farming and outbuildings, the whole surrounded by charming pleasure grounds, including pleasure gardens, tennis lawn, ornamental lake and boathouse, rockeries and waterfalls, kitchen gardens and meadows . . ."

In 1874 Galsworthy senior had moved his family to Coombe Leigh, the mansion he had just completed next door. Here the young John Galsworthy spent ten years of his childhood. The tennis courts where he played fierce tournaments against his brothers, the lawns where he staged mock battles, the orchard and stable block he visited each evening with his father, (all described in his sister's book, *Memories of John Galsworthy*) still survive, as do the little pond and grotto where he liked to sit. This house is still beautifully preserved as Holy Cross Convent School.

The last house to be built by Galsworthy senior was Coombe Croft. It survives, much as he knew it, as Rokeby School.

In 1887 the Galsworthys left Coombe. Their departure was a great loss to St John's Church, Kingston Vale, where the author was baptised and his father was a churchwarden, and to St Luke's Church, Kingston, which both his parents helped to establish in 1883.

But to return to Coombe Warren: the woman who made the house a byword in 19th and early 20th century society was Gladys Ripon, wife of the 2nd Marquess of Ripon. She was noted for her beauty, wit and love affairs. He, formerly Earl de Grey, was noted as the worst bore, but the finest shot, in England. His powerful appeal for his wife seems to have been that he enabled her to live a life devoted to pleasure, the arts and the spending of unlimited wealth.

Gladys Ripon was described by a contemporary as "tall and dark, a proud black swan who made any woman near her look pale." She was formerly Lady Constance Gladys Herbert, youngest daughter of Sidney Herbert. He became 1st Lord Herbert of Lea and died in 1861. Had he lived another year, he would have succeeded his half-brother, the 12th Earl of Pembroke. In the event, his two eldest sons successively became the 13th and 14th Earls, and Sidney Herbert's other children, including

Gladys, were granted precedence as children of an earl.

Gladys married the 4th Earl of Lonsdale in 1878. He died in 1882, aged 27, leaving her with an infant daughter. Three years later she married Earl de Grey, who became 2nd Marquess of Ripon in 1909, and the newly-weds settled in Coombe. Gladys re-named their house Coombe Court and extended it on a massive scale, virtually doubling the accommodation and adding a concert hall and ballroom.

She was a close friend of Edward VII and Queen Alexandra, and the chief patron of the London opera and ballet seasons. Consequently, her parties at Coombe Court were the most brilliant in Britain. Her friend and neighbour, Mrs Hwfa Williams, who lived at Coombe Springs nearby, has left descriptions of some of them in her book, *It Was Such Fun.*

She recalled an occasion when the Russian Ballet was taking London by storm and Lady Ripon brought the famous dancers Nijinsky and Karsavina to dine at Coombe Court and to meet Queen Alexandra and her sister, the Dowager Empress Marie.

> "After dinner Karsavina and her partner danced most exquisitely," writes Mrs Williams. "All Gladys's parties were divine. Sometimes she would bring all the opera artists down to Coombe Court and have wonderful parties. There would be Melba, Caruso and the de Reszkes, Plancon and others, and they used to sing divinely . . . never shall I forget the party she gave at Coombe Court when Pavlova, Nijinsky and the whole company was there."

The "proud black swan" died in 1917, leaving her husband to live in lonely splendour at Coombe Court with a butler, two footmen, a cook and a host of lesser fry to attend him. When he died, Coombe Court passed to his step-daughter, Lady Juliet Duff, and most of its old sparkle returned. She, like mother, loved a social whirl but, again like her mother, her second marriage was to a man who did not. In 1903 she had married Sir Robert Duff of the Life Guards, who was killed soon after the outbreak of war in 1914. In 1919 she married Major Keith Trevor; but the pair were divorced in 1926, whereupon she resumed her former name of Lady Juliet Duff.

Mr Francis Hodgson, was a gardener on the estate from 1920 until its break-up in 1931, and recalls parties there attended by the future George VI, The Queen of Spain, George V, Queen Mary, Sir Philip Sassoon and Lord Birkenhead.

The 1930's saw so much demolition and re-development in Kingston that the demise of some of the area's most stately homes passed without remark. Only the bulldozing of Coombe Court seems to have caused real sorrow.

"It is sad beyond words, because something is being taken from the fair county of Surrey which we can ill afford to part with," declared the Surrey Comet's leader column of August 15, 1931.

Today the spot where the mansion stood is occupied by two houses, Stone Garth and Coombe Crest; but most of the handsome boundary wall still runs along George Road. The original entrance and lodge is still there. The carriage drive, which once curved round to the stables, now leads to Robin Hill. This is a modern house, but surrounding it is much of the original landscaping, including a pond and statue fountain, the magnificent pillared pergola and the Italian garden, where royalty danced the night away by the glow of hundreds of lanterns.

A stroll down The Drive, cut through the grounds after the mansion was demolished, reveals more relics of a glamourous past. On the right are the steps used by some of the world's most distinguished feet on their way to play tennis on the courts that now form the gardens of 3 The Drive. Further down is the lovely lake, banked by rhododendrons, where Edward VII kept many a moonlight tryst in a little pavilion reached by a rustic bridge. Bridge and pavilion have gone now and the spot is covered by three houses.

* * * * * * * * *

Crossing the end of George Road is Warren Road, now one of the most expensive and elegant addresses in Britain. The houses are luxurious. The setting is as lovely as trees, shrubs and landscaping can make it. The golf course on the west side adds to the rural atmosphere.

It is hard to imagine the spot as Kingstonians of the early 19th century knew it. Much of it was heathland, smothered in golden gorse. The rest was woodland, teeming with wildlife and a rare species of butterfly, not found anywhere else in Britain. It was one of Kingston's favourite playgrounds. At weekends, families came with picnic hampers and on public holidays bull fights, cockfights and bare-fist fights were held here before thousands of spectators.

On working days The Warren, as it was known, served a more practical purpose. An ancient track ran across it leading from Coombe House and Farm to the highest point on Kingston Hill, and then on through Richmond Park to Richmond and the Thames. It was an invaluable short cut for people travelling to and from Richmond, Merton, Wimbledon and Kingston. Calico printers hurried along the track each day on their way from Merton to Wandsworth, and racegoers swarmed over by the thousand when Epsom meetings were on. Paupers struggled across the track en route from Wimbledon to their home parishes, while laden powder waggons lurched across the furze on their way to Putney from the gunpowder mills at Malden.

The Warren took on special significance in 1821 when its owner, Earl Spencer, gave part of it to the Government for the building of a semaphore station. This station was a relay point on the old communications system between the Admiralty in Whitehall and the fleets at Portsmouth. Though it remained in use for only a few decades, it is still remembered in the name Telegraph Cottage. This house is not, as often supposed, part of the old signal station. That stood on the opposite side of the lane and has long since disappeared. But the house is interesting in its own right as the home of General Eisenhower during World War II.

In 1837, as already mentioned, the entire Coombe Estate, including The Warren, was bought by the Duke of Cambridge. Kingston watched uneasily as he had boards put up forbidding anyone to cross the land. A big protest petition was organised, and for the next few years people were allowed free use of the track. In 1850, to the dismay of everyone, the Duke put ornamental gates across the entrance to The Warren and set a man on guard there.

A howl of fury went up, but before anything could be done, the Duke died. Indignation was forthwith transferred to his son and heir, the 2nd Duke.

Alderman Frederick Gould, at that time the most prominent public figure in Kingston, went to the gate and demanded to be let through. The gatekeepr retorted that the Duke's orders were to admit "respectable" people only and Alderman Gould, shaking with rage, went back to report the incident to the Kingston Board of Surveyors, which at that time controlled all the local highways. The Board demanded a personal confrontation with the Duke, and a special deputation was duly invited to St James's Palace.

The Duke was very polite, but very firm. He was willing, he said, to let "respectable" people through, but if all and sundry were admitted it would frighten the wildlife and spoil his shooting.

The Board of Surveyors were so incensed that they opened a public fund, raised £200 and decided to take the Duke to trial at the Summer Assizes in Croydon.

The result was a miniature civil war in Kingston. One half of the town thought it was disgraceful that a royal Duke and a great local benefactor should be treated in such a way. The other half declared that The Warren was a vital part of everyday life. Angry meetings were held. Strongly-worded posters and leaflets were printed.

Hodgson's Kingston Brewery was a major employer in 19th and 20th century Kingston.
In 1971 its disused buildings were destroyed by fire and replaced by today's shops, offices and multi-storey car park.

Eden Street/Clarence Street junction circa 1870.

The same spot in 1984.

The Kingston/Richmond horse bus outside the Druid's Head in Kingston Market Place.
The same spot in the 1980's.

The junction of Brook Street and Penrhyn Road (formerly Grove Lane) looked vastly different in the 19th century from now. The picturesque watersplash was covered over by Bedelsford Bridge in 1938. Only the curve of the pavement (left) remains the same.

The view from Clattern Bridge was once a beauty of Kingston. Today a concrete "raft" covers the Hogsmill Stream and Kingston Police Station, built in 1968, dominates the scene.

Canbury Lodge before the railway cut through its gardens in the 1860's.

The Canbury Lodge site in 1984.

Old Wood Street.

Wood Street in 1984.

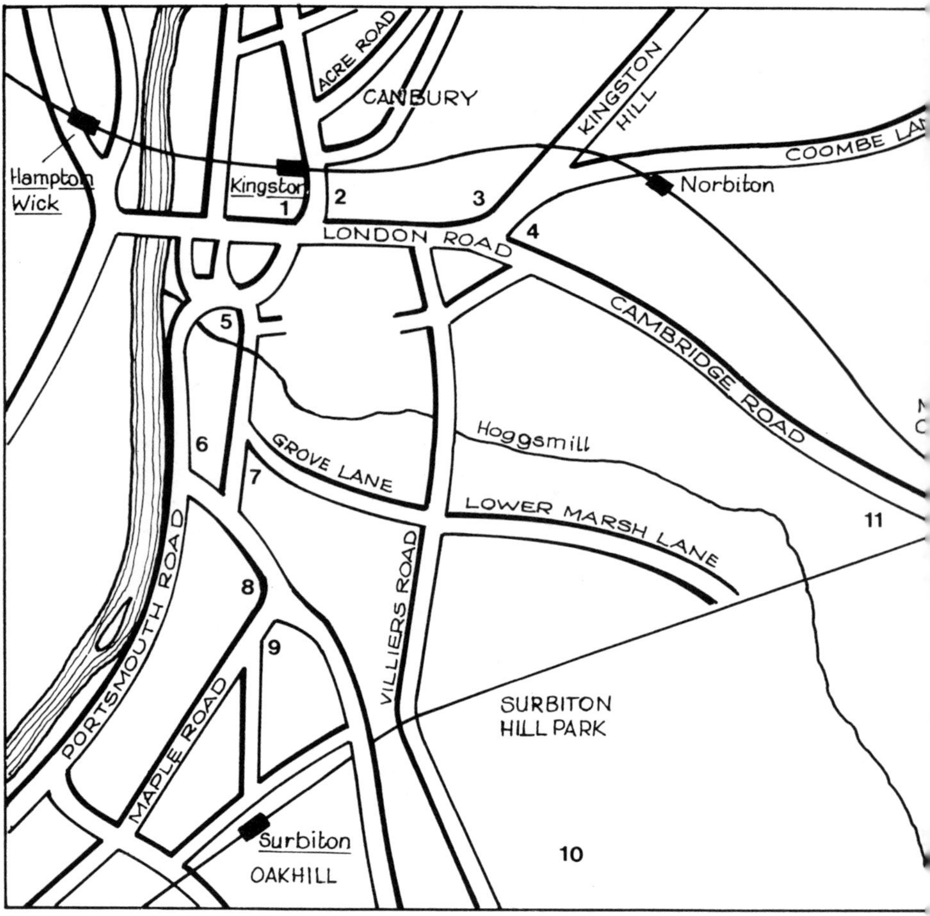

Key for Victorian Coombe (right)

1. Coombe Leigh (Now C. Ridge)
2. Coombe Court
3. Coombe Croft
4. Ballard Coombe
5. Coombe Springs
6. Coombe End
7. Coombe Warren
8. Coombe Cottage
9. Coombe House
10. Coombe House laundry
11. Coombe Hill Farm house
12. Coombe Lane Farm house
13. Union Workhouse

GC Golf Course

Scale:- 0 ¼ mile 500 m

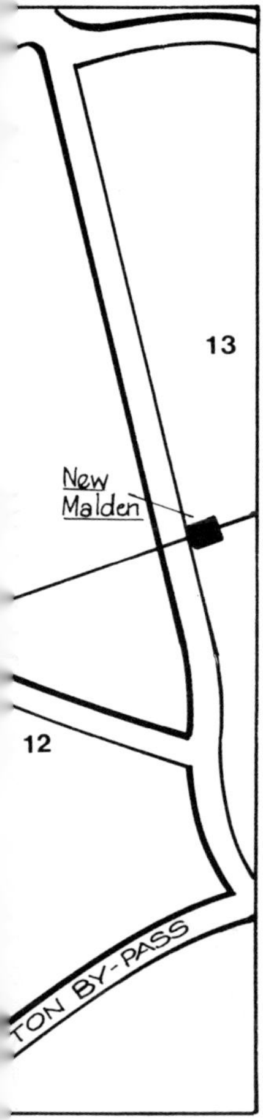

Left: Sketch plan showing new railways and old estates on the relevant roads.

Key:
1. Canbury House
2. Canbury Lodge (Croft)
3. Norbiton Hall
4. Norbiton Place
5. Kingston Hall
6. Woodbines
7. The Grove
8. Surbiton Hall
9. Elmers
10. Berrylands Farm
11. Norbiton Common Farm
12. Waitelands Farm
13. Hoppingwood Farm

Scale:-

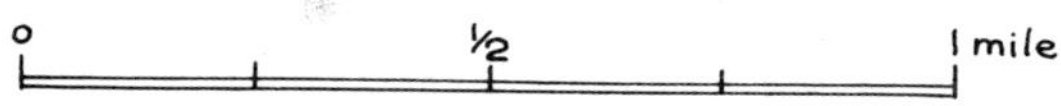

Below: Part of Victorian Coombe on the modern road plan.

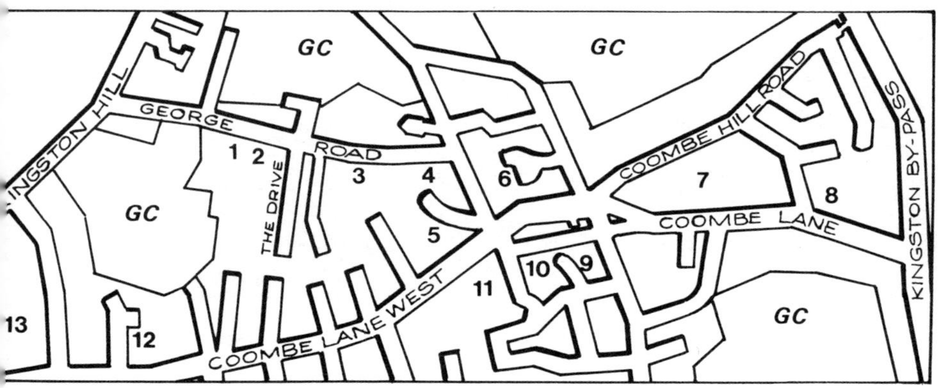

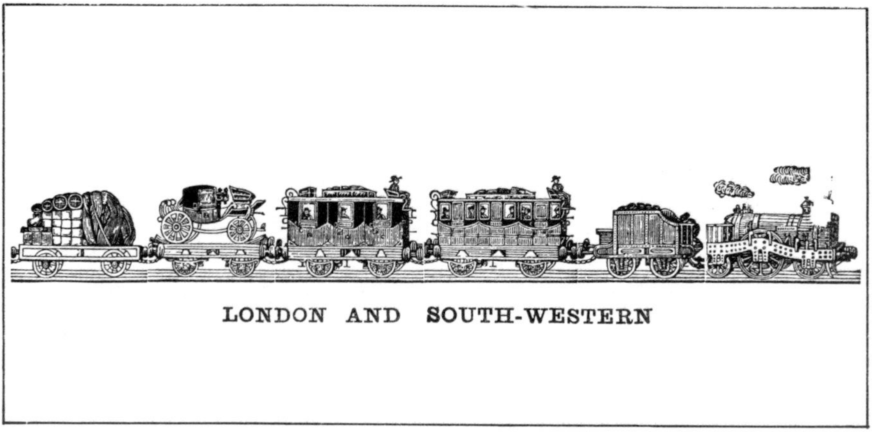

One of the first trains to serve the station at Kingston-on-Railway (Surbiton).

Kingston-on-Railway's first station, pictured circa 1838.

1st, 2nd and 3rd class passengers boarding the train to Kingston in 1847 en route to Epsom Races. (Courtesy of Illustrated London News)

Kingston Station in 1863.

Kingston Station in 1984.

Old Surbiton Station.

Modern Surbiton Station

Old Acre Road, drawn from Richmond Road, in the 1850's.
The house on the right is now a shop.

Modern Acre Road.

Old Eden Street.

Eden Street in 1984.

THE FILTERING-BASINS OF THE LAMBETH WATER COMPANY'S NEW WORKS, DITTON.

Lambeth Water Co's new filter beds in Portsmouth Road, 1852.

Norbiton Place circa 1828.

The trial opened in August 1853, and long lines of coaches left Kingston at dawn, full of townspeople eager to secure good seats in the public gallery. The Duke himself was enraged by the affair, even though a "special jury of Gentlemen" had been selected for the occasion.

The Board had done its work well. A long stream of witnesses went into the box, from illiterate labourers to influential gentlemen, each testifying that The Warren had been a right of way from time immemorial.

Gould appeared bearing a map of 1727, clearly showing The Warren as a public throughway, and thus disproving the Duke's contention that the way had only been made public with the opening of the semaphore station, and that when it closed the right of way ceased.

Finally, the judge declared he would hear no further witnesses, though several more were waiting in the wings. After a two-day hearing the "special jury of Gentlemen" gave its verdict: the public was entitled to unrestricted use of The Warren as a footpath, but not as a carriage-way.

The Duke was ordered to pay all the costs of the action. He was so incensed that he refused to play any part in Kingston's public life for some years afterwards.

Meanwhile the Board, with a fine sense of showmanship, despatched a pigeon from Croydon Assize Courts to carry news of the victory to Kingston. There was immediate rejoicing. Church bells pealed, bunting was hung and a brass band was hastily hired to meet the Surveyors and play them back to Kingston. Vast crowds also set out to welcome them. When the Surveyors finally came into Coombe Lane, they were escorted across The Warren to the gate on Kingston Hill, and the lock was removed amid shouts of triumph. Then the cavalcade made its way back to Kingston amid scenes of the wildest elation.

The affair was reported in *The Times* and became nationally known as The Battle of Coombe Warren. And now? Ironically The Warren, or Warren Road as it now is, still has a gate, sometimes guarded by a uniformed official, and opened to vehicle traffic as he thinks fit. But he has no jurisdiction over the little path that runs up beside the gate. Thanks to The Battle of Coombe Warren, the road is a public right of way to pedestrians, providing a direct route from Coombe Lane to Kingston Hill and saving what would otherwise be a long and tiring detour.

* * * * * * * * *

Entering Warren Road from Coombe Lane West, one cannot but admire a beautiful little cottage on the right. This, a former lodge, is all that remains of Coombe End. The mansion was the home of the Earls of Tankerville for many years, its 21 acres occupying the north side of Coombe Lane from Warren Road to a point opposite Traps Lane. In an auction sale advertisement of May 1882 it was described as a mansion with a carriage drive through finely timbered grounds, and boasting 17 bed and dressing rooms, a "suite of elegantly decorated reception rooms communicating together, 57 feet long", stabling for eight horses, walled kitchen garden, vineries, peach houses, terrace and two cottages. The land was held on lease from the Duke of Cambridge for 80 years.

Almost opposite stand the lodges and part of the impressive curved carriageway to Ballard Coombe, whose grounds once occupied the entire West side of Warren Road from its Coombe Lane entrance to George Road. The beautifully preserved mansion is now Marymount International School, but most of its acres have been given up to luxurious modern housing. Former aristocratic owners included Earl Listowel.

* * * * * * * * *

On the level stretch of road beyond the summit of Kingston Hill is an opening on the south side, flanked by pillars. It is now the entrance to Coombe Ridings, a private housing estate. Formerly, though, it was the entrance to Coombe Wood Nursery, and what is now the roadway was an avenue of some of the noblest conifers in the British Isles. It led to gardens containing such splendours as a rose garden featuring 500 different roses; a holly grove, containing no fewer than 36 species, and a host of trees and shrubs never seen in this country before.

The story of this place began in 1863, when a noted horticulturist named James Veitch acquired 35 acres of undulating Coombe woodland from the Duke of Cambridge. Here he created his world-famous Coombe Wood Nursery, which opened to the public in the autumn of 1865 "for free inspection and promenade at all times."

From here, members of the Veitch family made hazardous expeditions to places still virtually unknown to Europeans, risking their lives to bring back plants and seeds that were to revolutionise British gardening. Veitch explorers ultimately introduced to Britain 118 exotic ferns, 232 orchids, 498 herbaceous plants and 37 bulbs. The Veitch family ran Coombe Wood Nursery until 1914. Then it was acquired by Arthur Luff and Sons, and continued as a nursery until the early 1950's, when it was sold as building land.

However, one section of James Veitch's original nursery still survives as a glorious memorial. It is the Japanese water garden he laid out shortly after acquiring his Coombe site. Inspired by the famous Willow Pattern design, he created a series of lakes, linked by a stream fed from one of Coombe's many underground springs. He then added Japanese-style bridges, sculptures and summer houses, surrounded by rare trees, shrubs and ferms. Today the trees have matured and the scene is even more beautiful than in Veitch's day.

The fact that it still survives to give pleasure to thousands of people every year is due to Imperial Chemical Industries, who own it now, and a Victorian banker named Hugh Hammersley.

In 1865 Mr Hammersley acquired 13 acres from the Duke of Cambridge, and on it built his country mansion, Warren House. When he came to lay out the gardens he found that a section of Veitch's Nursery cut across his grounds, practically dividing them. Eventually, after much pleading by Mr Hammersley, James Veitch agreed to sell this part of the nursery so it could form an integral part of the Warren House estate.

It included the Japanese water garden, which is still immaculately maintained and still noted internationally for the rarity of its trees and shrubs.

After Hugh Hammersley's death in 1880, Warren House stood empty until 1884, when it was acquired by a prominent Liberal and banker, George Grenfell Glyn, 2nd Baron Wolverton.

Lord Wolverton was a close business associate of two of his neighbours – Bertram Currie at Coombe Warren and Edward Baring, later Lord Revelstoke, at Coombe Cottage. In 1864 the Currie family's banking business had amalgamated with Lord Wolverton's family firm, Glyn Mills and Co., a forerunner of today's Williams and Glyn's Bank. Both Currie and Wolverton were involved in many transactions with Baring's Bank, and during the famous Baring crisis of 1890, it was Currie who came to the rescue. Wolverton and Currie were also both dedicated Liberals, and both on close terms with Prime Minister Gladstone, who often visited them at their respective homes at Coombe.

Warren House was a favourite haunt of the Royal family from the time it was first built, Royals making frequent private visits there during the time of the Hammersleys, the Wolvertons and the Pagets, who acquired it in 1907.

Lord Wolverton died suddenly in 1887, leaving the then enormous fortune of £2m. His widow continued to live at Warren House until her death 10 years later. In Kingston she is remembered chiefly for the spire of St Luke's Church, which was the highest structure ever built in the Royal Borough when she provided it in 1894. Wolverton Avenue, off

Kingston Hill, was also named in her honour.

The Paget family occupied Warren House until 1954, when ICI bought the estate from Dame Leila Paget. Sir Arthur Paget made many additions to the house. They included a magnificent ballroom, built to celebrate the coronation of George V; the Persian Room, the winter garden and the Italian-style loggia.

If Gladstone, Edward VII, George V or the many other famous guests who frequented Warren House returned to it today, they would find it virtually unchanged. ICI, who use it for residential training courses, have made a point of maintaining it in all its original beauty, including the white marble bathroom, installed as part of the Royal suite on the first floor.

The gardens remain unspoiled, and are regularly opened by ICI so that the public can enjoy a living memento of 19th century Coombe at its stateliest.

* * * * * * * * *

Some of Coombe's stately homes were settings for entertainments and high living on an almost breathtaking scale. Some were so sober people virtually forgot their existence. Others were occupied by men of high intellect who, while choosing a life of exemplary quiet and rectitude, chose to live it in the most exquisite surroundings their wealth could buy. Coombe Warren came into this last category. It was built by the brilliant international banker and financier Bertram Wodehouse Currie as the Victorian ideal of a country home. Certainly it was loved by William Ewart Gladstone, who served four terms as Prime Minister and was a close friend of Mr Currie.

The Coombe Warren grounds formed a triangle bounded by what today are Coombe Hill Road, Coombe Lane West and Beverley Lane. The mansion itself was built early in the 1860's as an exuberant blend of farm cottages and Tudor palace, with clusters of low gables, oriel windows and heavy chimneys, offset by a massive square tower. Mr Currie's country idyll was rudely interrupted. Soon after its completion the mansion was destroyed by fire, and in 1870 he had to embark on a complete rebuild. The result was the house which at times was the seat of Liberal government in Gladstone's days of power. Both the first and second mansions were designed by George Devey, famous in the 19th century for his development of domestic architecture.

The red brick boundary walls still survive in Coombe Lane West and Coombe Hill Road. Behind them Government decisions were formulated which still have a powerful influence on life today.

It was Gladstone, for example, who carried through reforms such as the introduction of elementary education for all, votes by ballot, the abolition of the purchase of Army commissions and of religious tests in universities. However, he never achieved his most ardent wish: the introduction of home rule for Ireland. Twice he fought to get the Bill through. Twice he failed, resigning from office after each defeat.

Much of the thinking behind these reforms was carried out at Coombe Warren, where Gladstone loved to get up at dawn and wander through the grounds, often in deep conversation with Bertram Currie.

They thought alike on most things. It has been said of Gladstone that "his long life was one of moral stature and increasing advocary of liberal causes." The same was true of Currie – so much so that when he accepted the High Stewardship of Kingston in 1893, he made it plain that he did so only because Kingston Corporation was not given to the self-indulgent feasting and drinking practised in other boroughs.

Certainly he backed Gladstone every inch of the way in his long career, placing Coombe Warren at his disposal when he was ill in 1884 and giving over his dining room for meetings of the Cabinet.

A big event in Kingston's Victorian calendar was the day Currie entertained 4,000 local Liberals to a garden party at Coombe Warren. The *Kingston and Surbiton News* gave a glowing description of house and garden, ending thus: ". . . of the grounds it is impossible to speak in language of too rosey a hue.

"The infinite variety of scene, the numerous walks, the luxuriant foliage, the majestic trees, the verdant lawns, the lovely flowers and the commanding prospect."

A touching tribute to Currie's regard for Gladstone was the little stone temple he had built in his gardens. In it was a sandstone bust of the Liberal leader, crowned with a wreath of bay leaves.

Gladstone retired from the premiership at the age of 85, but his closing years were darkened by the loss of his friend, Bertram Currie, who died in 1896. Two years later, Gladstone too was dead.

The influence of both men is still apparent today. The whole world knows of Gladstone. Currie is little known, but his outlook on life is reflected in the many surviving remnants of Coombe Warren. Currie's only son, Laurence, sold Coombe Warren in 1926 for £24,000. The mansion was demolished, and its 18 acres divided into building plots; but the decorative walling, the temple, gateways, lodges, magnificent orangery and other flights of Victorian gothic fancy, designed by the eminent architect George Devey, remain in such profusion that they still enable one to savour the essence of gentlemanly life in 19th century

Coombe. Indeed, the orangery was added to the Department of the Environment's list of historic buildings in 1983.

Bertram Currie's beliefs are also represented in the handsome Roman Catholic Church of St Agatha which his widow, Caroline, built in King's Road, Kingston in his memory.

* * * * * * * * *

Lord Chancellor Walk, on the north side of Coombe Lane West, now covers the site of Coombe Springs. Only the lodge remains, together with the gateway through which passed practically every name of note in the Victorian and Edwardian social calendar.

It was long the home of Mr and Mrs Hwfa Williams. He was the man who transformed Sandown Park from a country estate at Esher into a racecourse. There was no other course so near, or so accessible to London. Williams' stroke of business genius was so successful that it led to the establishment of other suburban racecourses, such as Hurst Park and Kempton Park. These developments, as described elsewhere, added further weight to Kingston's already considerable social burdens.

Mrs Hwfa Williams had a lively personality that drew everybody who was anybody, together with many who were not, to her home at Coombe. "My own poor little Coombe Springs" was how she described the place, and indeed it was modest compared with its neighbours. The gardens had only six acres and the house only 13 bed and dressing rooms.

"There is absolutely no architecture about this place, and it was built apparently in 1840," writes Mrs Williams in her memoirs, "Evidently the architect was so proud of himself that he put the date on a stone tablet outside the house. It was quite inexcusable that it should be so ugly because we have two lovely Tudor well-houses to copy from on the property, built in the time of Cardinal Wolsey . . . friends used to marvel how we could possibly live in such an ugly house."

Among the weekend guests who flocked regularly to Coombe Springs were King Edward VII, Prince Felix Youssoupoff (later to enter history as the murderer of Rasputin) and celebrities such as Nellie Melba and Anna Pavlova.

Mrs Williams organised the opening of Coombe Woods golf course, whose beautiful wooded acres have been a major factor in preserving Coombe as one of the three loveliest and most sought-after addresses within the London area.

She asked the Prime Minister, Arthur Balfour, to open the course in 1905.

"Dear Mr Balfour . . . he was always so kind and put himself out to oblige his friends. Though he could with difficulty spare the time, he came down to luncheon, which we had out of doors. Prince Francis of Teck, Sir Edward Vincent and several others came, and after luncheon we went to the first green, where quite a crowd of people had come out from Kingston to see Mr Balfour drive from the first tee. As bad luck would have it, he sliced the first ball and drove it into the rough."

It was of no significance.

"I am glad to say that he brought luck to the little golf course, which has flourished ever since," wrote the exhuberant Mrs Williams.

* * * * * * * * *

Kingston has a unique link with the Princess of Wales. It is Coombe Cottage, a rambling old house hidden behind trees just off the Kingston By-pass.

It is not, despite its name, a cottage. It has more than 60 rooms and no fewer than 40 separate roofs. Neither, despite its aristocratic past, is it a grand or a beautiful place. Homely is the word that springs most readily to mind.

That is exactly what the Princess's great-great-grandfather intended when he created this country retreat for his bride in the early 1860's.

He was Edward Charles Baring, head of the mercantile firm of Baring Bros. In 1861 he married Louisa Bulteel, grand-daughter of the 2nd Earl Grey, who was Britain's Prime Minister from 1830 to 1834. The newly-weds needed a country home where they could escape the pressures of London and, they hoped bring up a family. They found it in Coombe Cottage.

Edward Baring more than doubled the size of the house. He also added a tower and a fanciful little stable clock in mock-Tudor style. The work was completed in 1863, and proudly he had his initials and the date set into the stable wall in memory of his handiwork. This inscription still survives.

The Barings had six children during their years at Coombe Cottage. it was their younger daughter Margaret, born in 1868, who established the links with the Princess of Wales. In 1887 she married the Hon. Charles Spencer and embarked on a life of childbearing and selfless good works. She thrived on the good works. The childbearing killed her.

She was only 38 when she died in the summer of 1906 after giving birth to her sixth baby. Her husband ultimately became the 6th Earl Spencer and, through their son, great-grandfather of our Princess of Wales. The selfless Margaret is not forgotten. A portrait drawing of her is prominently desplayed in the family sitting room at Althorp, the Spencer seat.

In 1881 Edward Baring invited the widowed and exiled Empress Eugenie to make her home at Coombe Cottage after the shattering loss of her only son. She remained there a year, recovering her strength and was frequently visited there by Queen Victoria and the rest of the Royal family.

In 1885, when Edward Baring became first Baron Revelstoke, the London and South Western Railway announced plans to build a railway line close to the Coombe Cottage estate. The new Lord Revelstoke was outraged at the prospect of losing the quiet surroundings he had savoured for nearly a quarter of a century. He made the railway company buy the whole estate for a huge price and used the proceeds to build himself another rural retreat in Devon.

As it happened, the railway line was never completed. A start was made and a bridge and part of a line built. They are still visible, just off the Kingston By-pass. Then the scheme was abandoned, leaving the company with an estate it did not want and on which it had no hope of re-couping financially. It stayed empty for years until tenanted by, among others, the legendary Dame Nellie Melba. She loved it so much that when she returned to her native Australia she named her home there Coombe Cottage, in memory of what she described as the happiest days of her life.

Coombe Cottage survives amid a tiny fraction of its original grounds. Now, however, it is the home of the Rediffusion company.

* * * * * * * * *

Kenry House and its next door neighbour, Coombe Hurst, are today part of Kingston Polytechnic; but orginally they were luxurious country houses, whose origins are traced in L.E. Gent's *The Manor of Coombe or Coombe Nevill,* published by Kingston Upon Thames Archaeological Society in 1979.

Kenry House was built shortly after William Ogle Hunt had leased 25 acres of the Coombe Estate from the 2nd Earl Spencer in 1832 Mr Hunt, a solicitor, lived in the house until the early 1850's. Originally it was known as Coombe Wood. From 1874, local directories list it as Kenry House, and show the Earl of Dunraven as the occupant until 1926.

The Dunraven peerage was an Irish one; but the 3rd Earl was created Baron Kenry in the UK. When he died in 1871, he was succeeded by his son, Windham. The barony became extinct after his death in 1926, but is remembered in the name of his house.

The adjoining mansion, Coombe Hurst, was built on 43 acres of land leased by Samuel Smith from the 3rd Earl Spencer in 1835. Mr Smith, described in Census returns as a barrister, examiner of Petitions of Private Bills at the House of Commons, and a Surrey County magistrate, lived in the house until his death in 1881 at the age of 86.

His chief interest today is that he was an uncle of Florence Nightingale. His sister, Fanny, was the mother of Florence and her sister, Parthenope. His wife, Mary, was a sister of Florence and Parthenope's father. The girls were frequent guests at Coombe Hurst, and the Census returns show Parthenope was staying there in 1841.

After Samuel Smith's death, the house was occupied by Henry Vyner and then, from 1885, by Capt. R.C. de Grey Vyner, grandson of the 1st Earl de Grey, and brother-in-law of the Marquis of Ripon. He owned race horses, stud farms and 26,700 acres of land, and Coombe Hurst was but one of his five residences. Captain Vyner died in 1915. Thereafter, Coombe Hurst appears to have remained empty until 1923, and the arrival of Baron de Forest, a baron of the old Austrian Empire and a Liberal MP.

Accordng to the *Surrey Comet* of June 24, 1933, the house would have been demolished but for the intervention of Mr S.E. Parkes, chairman of Wandsworth Greyhound Stadium. He bought the property and had it extensively modernised.

* * * * * * * * *

There had been a manor house in Coombe since Elizabethan times; but the mansion still remembered by older Kingstonians is the replacement, built in the mid-18th century.

This palatial white building, with its Tuscan portico, stood near the junction of Coombe Lane West with Traps Lane. Its Tudor boundary wall still survives in Traps Lane, and one of the lodges still stands guard at what was once the principal entrance in Coombe Lane West. In what was formerly some 40 acres of garden and parkland is part of the stabling, together with the old dairy and laundry. The house itelf, however, has gone. In November 1932, developers Higgs and Hill announced they had bought 715 acres of the Coombe estate. The mansion, by then semi-derelict, was demolished the following year. On its site now are the neo-Georgian houses of Coombe House Chase, with

Fitzgeorge Avenue cutting through what was once the lawn. However, the beautiful lake remains. Fed by seven underground springs, it was close to the south front of the house, and a favourite feature of the grounds.

Contrary to local legend, neither the Earls Spencer nor the Dukes of Cambridge ever lived at Coombe House. Instead, as L.E. Gent describes in detail, the house was let to a succession of tenants. Most of them were Members of Parliament or peers; for Coombe, though rural, was within easy reach of Westminster.

Two Prime Ministers made their home at Coombe House. One was the Marquis of Rockingham, who was Premier in 1765/66, and again in 1782. The other was the 2nd Earl of Liverpool who, as Robert Banks Jenkinson, took a lease on the house in 1805 and died there in 1828.

He had served as Prime Minister from 1812 to the year before his death. During his tenancy some of the world's most famous people visited Coombe House, including the Duke of Wellington, who stayed there in August 1814 en route to the Netherlands and Victory at Waterloo. Other guests were the Emperor Alexander of Russia, the King of Prussia, General Blucher and General Platoff.

Later, Queen Victoria became fond of Coombe House. She came there first in 1861, and spent so much time delighting in the purity of the air that the lawns near the lake were always known afterwards as Queen's Walk. At the close of her visit she planted a tree which could still be there among the many other fine old trees that still survive from that era.

In July 1880, following the death of lessee Mr John Cosygarne Sim, Coombe House opened as a Hydropathic establishment, where Dr T.E. Foster MacGeogh offered Turkish and vapour baths, tepid and cold needle baths, spinal douches and mustard packs.

Evidently Dr MacGeough, who had run similar hydropathic establishments in Tunbridge Wells and Matlock, was well connected. The Prince and Princess of Wales headed the notable guests he entertained there during his seven-year tenure.

The *Kingston and Surbiton News* gave a description of the house and gardens during a garden party held there in the summer of 1883:

> "The rooms it contains seem almost innumerable, and all are lofty and well lighted and ventilated. In the music room there is a fine organ by Cramer . . . in close proximity to this is the dining hall in which cabinet meetings were formerly held. This opens into a conservatory containing plants of the choicest description. Further on is the Italian garden, in which there are a number of marble statues by celebrated

artists and, adjoining this, is the French garden, tastefully laid out with the choicest plants. The conservatories at the west end of the house are more than an acre in extent. These include a rosery, azalea and tropical houses, and a vinery containing a vine capable of growing a ton of grapes during the season. The lawn on the south side of the house is exceptionally beautiful, being shaded by fine trees and skirted by a small lake containing no less than seven springs. It was from these springs that Cardinal Wolsey first drew a supply of water for his palace at Hampton Court and they are used for the same purpose at the present time.

"The rose walk in front of the house is simply charming and it is no exaggeration to say that it would be difficult to find in the county of Surrey a more beautiful spot or more charming abode."

The Manor of Coombe no longer exists, but the area has never lost its ambience of luxury and high-class style. Today it is still one of the most prestigious addresses in Britain – and one of the most expensive.

* * * * * * * * * *

As the 19th century came to a close, Kingstonians could reflect that within less than an average lifespan, the railway revolution had altered social, economic and environmental patterns that had endured for centuries.

They might have hoped for a breathing space to come to terms with their new world. It was not to be. The 20th century had barely begun before the advent of tramways and the internal combustion engine heralded another 'all change' in England's oldest Royal Borough.

Our Sponsors

Every firm in Kingston aims to make a profit from operating here. That is what business is about. Some, however, are as committed to giving as they are to taking. All the businesses listed here have this and three other factors in common: each has helped to pay for the printing and binding of this book, each has special links with Victorian Kingston and each, in the contributions they make so generously to local community projects, is motivated by a genuine regard for Britain's oldest Royal Borough. We are fortunate indeed to have such firms in our midst:

AMARI, which originated as a tin-mining company in 1931, is now the major metal distributor in Britain and one of the fastest-growing metal companies in the world. In 1981 it moved to Kingston, setting up its headquarters in the historic riverside house at 52 High Street. in 1983 the company regained its independence from British Petroleum, who had acquired it three years earlier. Let by their managing director, Mr John Pither, staff found much of the cash required to buy back their company's freedom, with the result that many are now shareholders. Mr Pither and several of his team are natives of Surrey, with a deep interest in local history – of which their own building is a beautiful part.

ARMY AND NAVY'S department store in Kingston Market Place is the oldest retail firm in Kingston and one of the oldest in Britain. A linen drapery was established here in 1740 and has continued without a break under successive owners. During the 19th century it expanded on to what had been the site of the Castle Inn, and has carefully preserved the beautiful 17th century staircase of the inn as part of the store. Queen Victoria and many other members of the Royal family have been regular customers here.

ARROW PLASTICS: This firm is a unique bridge between one of Kingston's most modern local industries and one of its oldest. It was founded in 1946 by Commander Walter Paine and Mr Stanley Brain, and specialises in vacuum forming and extrusion. It is also a noted British pioneer in the use of plastics in lighting. Yet it has a strong sense of history and is conscious that its site in Hampden Road was originally Kingston Potteries, an old local industry which could rely on an abundance of clay when this now densely-built area consisted only of fields and common. As proof of its interest in local history, Arrow has not only given generously towards this book, but produces an annual calendar. It illustrates old Kingston and has become a sought-after collector's item.

BENTALLS: Frank Bentall took over a tiny, working-class drapery shop in Clarence Street in 1867. He, followed by his sons and grandsons, gradually developed it into one of the biggest and most prestigious department stores in Britain. Today Frank Bentall's great-grandsons are as actively concerned with the business as their forefathers, and the firm has achieved world-wide eminence for quality and its range of services, numbering Royalty among its regular customers. As well as making a vital contribution to Kingston's employment, trading and community life, the firm has branches at Ealing, Tunbridge Wells, Worthing and Bracknell.

BOOTS: Jesse Boot, a Nottingham farm labourer's son, opened his first drug and herbalists shop in 1877. When he died, 54 years later, there were more than a thousand Boots branches in Britain. Boots came to Kingston early in the 1900's, and showed their respect for its history by transforming the frontage of their Market Place premises into a beautiful carved and gilded record of Kingston's royal past. Late in 1984 Boots moved to splendid new premises built on part of the former site of the Surrey Comet. They commemorated this event, and their long trading history in Kingston, with a donation to this book.

GLEMBY: This world-famous firm was founded by Saul Glemby in 1883 as a hairnet manufactory. The first Glemby hairdressing salon opened in 1910. Ten years later the Finkelstein company merged with Glemby and the firm grew rapidly. There are now 1,300 Glemby salons throughout the world, and the second and third generations of Finkelstein are running the business. Glemby, which has 74 salons in the UK, came to Kingston in 1975, opening a salon within Bentalls. Though the company is so large, expanding at the rate of one new salon a week, it is still very much a family firm, concerned with contributing to each of the communities it serves. Its donation to this book was a token of thanks for achieving their first century.

GRIDLEY MISKIN: James Gridley set up his sawmill in Union Street, Kingston some 120 years ago, cutting and supplying timber to builders engaged in the great Victorian post-railway building boom. In 1872 he acquired the huge Bridge Barn adjoining Kingston Bridge and later, with his brother Frederick, built a sawmill in Water Lane. Both brothers died in 1920, and the following year their business was amalgamated with that of George Miskin, who had been involved in timber since 1885. In the 1960's Gridley Miskin's riverside premises in Kingston were cleared for re-development and the firm moved to the opposite bank of the river at Moira Wharf, Hampton Wick. It is now a subsidiary of the Sabah group, but is still proud of its deep local roots.

KINGSTON ESTATE DEVELOPERS: This family firm, founded by Mr Jack Hickman more than 50 years ago, has played a major part in the residential and commercial development of 20th century Kingston. At the same time, it has always maintained strong personal interest in the affairs and welfare of the area, setting new standards of commercial architecture designed to enhance the environment the Hickmans have known and loved for so long. The firm made its mark on social history by devising a scheme for buying flats on mortgage at a time when this advantage applied only to houses. The scheme, soon adopted by countless imitators, revolutionised home ownership in Britain.

LITTLEWOODS: John Moores founded this organisation in 1923 when he launched Littlewoods Pools. The mail order division was started in 1932, followed by the chain stores division in 1937. Littlewoods opened their Kingston store in 1961 and doubled its sales area in 1977. In 1984 the Kingston store was one of the first of the firm's 108 branches to be re-structured in keeping with a new, up-market trading policy. Littlewoods donation to this book commemorates this new development.

MARKS AND SPENCER: The firm goes back to 1884, when Michael Marks, a Polish refugee, set up a stall in Leeds Market selling articles at a penny each. Ten years later he was joined by Thomas Spencer, and one of the most famous retailing names in the world was born. Before World War I the partners had opened a Penny Bazaar at 15 Clarence Street, Kingston. In 1931 the firm moved to its present site at Clarence Street and the store, much enlarged in 1984, is an important factor in Kinston's well-being – not only in the commercial sense but in the support it gives to local projects.

OFFER GROUP: The firm's roots go back to the early 1860's when the Burgoine brothers established a boatbuilding business at 22 Kingston High Street and, later, on the riverside at Hampton Wick. In the meantime, James Offer had started business in Kingston as a gas, electricity and sanitary engineer. The Burgoine and Offer families became linked by marriage. H.J. Offer eventually acquired the Burgoine property, and gradually extended activities to building, property investment and management. In the 1950's the firm formed a number of companies, some engaged in investment and some in trading, under the name of the Offer Group. The Offer family continue to live in and around Kingston and maintain a close interest in its welfare.

FREDK. W. PAINE: Of all the businesses in the Royal Borough, none has made a greater contribution to local amenities than the firm established by Fredk. W. Paine's father in New Malden in 1884. From humble beginnings, Fredk. W. established branches of his funeral business in most of the expanding localities of the South East. When he died in 1945 he was owner of the largest concern of its kind in the country. His firm lives on as a family-run organisation which makes a point of contributing generously but unostentatiously to the Royal Borough where it was born and where it still keeps its headquarters.

SALAMANDER INVESTMENTS: This young company was born in 1979, the offspring of the Offer Group and Nigel Dearsley. It is concerned with commercial development, and combines Offer's long experience in building and investment with Nigel Dearsley's commercial expertise. Though such a forward-looking company, Salamander has genuine interest and pride in the local past. In developments such as the Crown Arcade in Kingston, and the transformation of the historic Old Crown from a public house into shops and flats, its aim is to provide the best of modern commercial buildings while conserving the most valuable and beautiful features of the past.

Further substantial donations towards this book have been made by **Mr Alexander Georgiados** and the **Kingston Lottery**. Mr Georgiados' home was once a part of Coombe's stateliest and most luxurious mansions, Coombe Warren, designed by the eminent Victorian architect, George Devey. The mansion disappeared in 1927, but Mr Georgiados' home retains the beautiful orangery that was said to represent Devey's best work.

Kingston Lottery was launched by the Council in December 1977 and is acknowledged as the best of all the civic lottery schemes in Greater London. Over the past seven years it has raised some half-million pounds, using the money to help provide a host of amenities, ranging from Kingston's riverside walk to an ambulance for the Multiple Sclerosis Society.

Erratum:
On page 143 In 1865 Malden and Coombe,... should read:

In 1965 Malden and Coombe, together with Surbiton were amalgamated to form the Royal Borough of Kingston upon Thames.

Index of Names

To save space, most places outside Kingston are omitted; churches, public houses, and railway stations are grouped under the appropriate headings.

Abbreviations: Kingston – K; New Malden – NM; Surbiton – S.